ELECTRICIANS

PRACTICAL CAREER GUIDES

Series Editor: Kezia Endsley

Clean Energy Technicians, Marcia Santore
Computer Game Development & Animation, by Tracy Brown Hamilton
Craft Artists, by Marcia Santore
Criminal Justice Professionals, by Kezia Endsley
Culinary Arts, by Tracy Brown Hamilton
Dental Assistants and Hygienists, by Kezia Endsley
Education Professionals, by Kezia Endsley
Electricians, by Marcia Santore
Fine Artists, by Marcia Santore
First Responders, by Kezia Endsley
Health and Fitness Professionals, by Kezia Endsley
Information Technology (IT) Professionals, by Erik Dafforn
Mathematicians and Statisticians, by Kezia Endsley
Media and Journalism Professionals, by Tracy Brown Hamilton
Medical Office Professionals, by Marcia Santore
Multimedia and Graphic Designers, by Kezia Endsley
Nursing Professionals, by Kezia Endsley
Plumbers, by Marcia Santore
Skilled Trade Professionals, by Corbin Collins
Veterinarian Technicians and Assistants, by Kezia Endsley

ELECTRICIANS

A Practical Career Guide

MARCIA SANTORE

ROWMAN & LITTLEFIELD
Lanham • Boulder • New York • London

Published by Rowman & Littlefield
An imprint of The Rowman & Littlefield Publishing Group, Inc.
4501 Forbes Boulevard, Suite 200, Lanham, Maryland 20706
www.rowman.com

6 Tinworth Street, London, SE11 5AL, United Kingdom

Copyright © 2021 by The Rowman & Littlefield Publishing Group, Inc.

All rights reserved. No part of this book may be reproduced in any form or by any electronic or mechanical means, including information storage and retrieval systems, without written permission from the publisher, except by a reviewer who may quote passages in a review.

British Library Cataloguing in Publication Information Available

Library of Congress Cataloging-in-Publication Data Available

Names: Santore, Marcia, 1960– author.
Title: Electricians : a practical career guide / Marcia Santore.
Description: Lanham, Maryland : Rowman & Littlefield, [2021] | Series: Practical career guides | Includes bibliographical references. | Summary: "Electricians: A Practical Career Guide includes interviews with professionals in a field that has proven to be a stable, lucrative, and growing profession. If you're looking for a career as an electrician this is the book for you."—Provided by publisher.
Identifiers: LCCN 2020053417 (print) | LCCN 2020053418 (ebook) | ISBN 9781538152034 (paperback) | ISBN 9781538152041 (epub)
Subjects: LCSH: Electrical engineering—Vocational guidance. | Electrical engineers.
Classification: LCC TK159 .S27 2021 (print) | LCC TK159 (ebook) | DDC 621.3023—dc23
LC record available at https://lccn.loc.gov/2020053417
LC ebook record available at https://lccn.loc.gov/2020053418

∞™ The paper used in this publication meets the minimum requirements of American National Standard for Information Sciences—Permanence of Paper for Printed Library Materials, ANSI/NISO Z39.48-1992.

Contents

Introduction

So You Want a Career as an Electrician

Welcome to a career as an electrician!

- Do you like to work with your hands?
- Are you careful and precise?
- Do you like to figure things out and solve problems?
- Do you like to help people?
- Do you want to earn a good income right away?
- Do you want a job that will *always* be needed?

If you answered "Yes!" to these questions, you might want to be an electrician.

As an electrician, you'll help people, solve problems, and make a great living. *michaeljung/iStock/Getty Images*

Electricians belong to the type of career known as "skilled trades." Because of the big push for everyone to go to four-year colleges over the last few decades, the trades have become neglected as careers for younger people. But these are great jobs! Right now—as we enter the third decade of the new millennium—there are more than 500,000 open trades jobs in the United States.

All of these skilled trades jobs pay well. And you can learn the skills of your trade in less time than it takes to earn a bachelor's degree because in-class learning is only part of the way you learn a trade. The most important way you learn is through an apprenticeship with a master tradesperson.

Think about that. Instead of taking out student loans to go to four years of college, you could be getting paid to be an apprentice for the same amount of time. *Hmmm*. And the coursework that you do need to take is available at a much lower cost. (Check out the section about financial aid in chapter 3 of this book).

So why choose the trade of electrician? Because it's one of the most secure and one of the best paid.

Skilled trades jobs are mostly associated with building and construction and with maintenance and repair. Our society always needs people to do all of those jobs—but the need for some of them rises and falls with the needs of industry.

Electrical work is different. Everyone has electrical wiring in their homes and workplaces, so everyone needs an electrician at one time or another. Everyone. Always. So the demand for qualified electricians goes up, but it never goes down.

Okay, so you get great pay and job security. That's fine. But is that all there is? What about that feeling that you're doing something that matters? What about a sense of accomplishment? What about making a difference in the world?

Great news! Electricians can have all those things, too! As an electrician, you will have the chance to make a real difference to people who really need you.

Careers for Electricians

Electrician careers are everywhere. Wherever you live or want to live, whatever type of electrician you decide to become, there is a job already waiting for you.

- Before you earn your electrician's license, you can have a job immediately as an apprentice, learning the trade from a master electrician.

- After you earn your journey-level electrician's license, you'll be able to be hired as a full-fledged electrician and work on electrical jobs as part of a team.
- Soon, you'll earn your master electrician's license (also called an electrical contractor license) and have apprentice and journey-level electricians working for you.

The Market Today

The demand for skilled tradespeople in every field is very high, and the demand for electricians is definitely one of the most needed. According to the U.S. Bureau of Labor Statistics, the job outlook for electricians is excellent, with jobs expected to grow by around 8 percent between 2019 and 2029—much higher than the national average.

Not only are new electrician jobs being created every day, but many current electricians are retiring or planning to retire soon. More electricians will be needed to replace these skilled tradespeople and to be ready to train the next generation that comes along after you.

What Does This Book Cover?

In this book, you'll get a general overview of what different kinds of electricians do and what to expect at different stages of your career as an electrician. Each chapter represents a step in your journey.

STEP 1: WHY CHOOSE A CAREER AS AN ELECTRICIAN?

In the first chapter, you'll learn about a few of the types of electrician jobs that are out there. In this book, we'll focus on the following:

- Residential electricians
- Commercial electricians
- Electrical contractors
- Electrical inspectors

You'll get a good idea of what each type of electrician does, required skills, working conditions, work schedule, and what you could expect to earn in each of those jobs. You'll also learn a little bit about jobs that are similar to electricians or that use some of the same skills.

Step 1 is where you'll find more information about the steps to becoming an electrician: apprentice, journey level, and master.

STEP 2: FORMING A CAREER PLAN

The second chapter is all about you and how you can plan a career as an electrician. What do you need to know about yourself? How can you make your time in high school work for you? Where can you find more information? How can you plan to earn your electrician's license? How do things work in different parts of the country? Having a plan helps keep you on the right track toward your goals!

STEP 3: PURSUING THE EDUCATION PATH

Electricians learn the skills of their trade through coursework and apprenticeships. Some programs offer diplomas or associate degrees. You'll also need continuing education hours to stay current and to maintain your license at the journeyman and master levels. The third chapter of this book is all about the ins and outs of getting the best education you can at the lowest cost. Scholarships abound!

STEP 4: WRITING YOUR RÉSUMÉ AND INTERVIEWING

In the fourth chapter, you'll learn about finding, applying for, and keeping a job as an electrician. Do you need a résumé? What should it look like? You'll also find out how to write a cover letter, fill in an application form, and interview like a pro.

Where Do You Start?

As a licensed electrician, you have many opportunities. Take the first step toward your future.

1

Why Choose a Career as an Electrician?

What Is an Electrician?

An electrician is a skilled tradesperson who installs and repairs electrical wiring or any kind of electrical system. Electricians might work in homes, offices, institutions, or commercial buildings. They might specialize in the electrical systems of cars, boats, airplanes, or other systems such as HVAC, lighting, security, or computer networks.

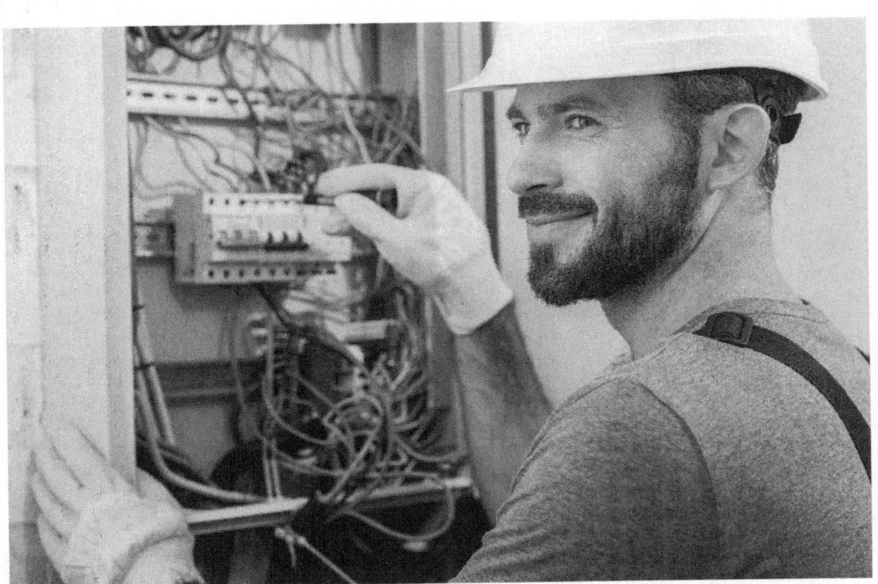

Being an electrician means having a highly paid job that's in high demand. *LightFieldStudios/iStock/Getty Images*

> Working as an electrician requires a strong work ethic and positive attitude to be successful. The work can be strenuous with long days on your feet.—Steve Schnute.[1]

What Skills Do Electricians Need?

As an electrician, you'll need certain skills and personal qualities to do the job.

KNOWLEDGE

- Math (including algebra)
- Electrical systems
- Mechanical systems
- Safety protocols and procedures
- Using tools and equipment—choosing the right ones for the job
- Reading and drawing electrical circuits

TECHNICAL SKILLS

- Reading blueprints and technical diagrams
- Installing and terminating low-voltage cable
- Maintaining wiring, control, and lighting systems
- Using testing devices to identify electrical problems
- Inspecting electrical components (e.g., transformers, circuit breakers)
- Wiring electrical circuits based on drawings/plans
- Fabricating electrical conduit runs by hand
- Using tools (hand and power) to repair or replace wiring, fixtures, or equipment

PERSONAL QUALITIES

- Good color vision to identify wires by color
- Good fine motor control for grasping and manipulating small objects
- Critical thinking skills to perform tests and understand the results

- Physical strength and stamina
- Troubleshooting and problem-solving skills
- Ability to work independently or as part of a team
- People skills to work with customers and coworkers
- Communication skills to direct and train workers assisting with electrical jobs

Anything Else?

To work as an electrician, you'll most likely have to meet these criteria, as well as the skills listed previously:

- Age eighteen or older
- High school diploma, GED, or more education
- Valid driver's license
- Dependable transportation
- Appropriate electrician's license (apprentice, journey level, master—we'll get to that later in this chapter)

WHAT TOOLS DO ELECTRICIANS USE?

Although the tools electricians use vary with their specialties, in general, you'll most likely be using a combination of hand and power tools, including:

- Ammeter
- Cable testers
- Conduit benders
- Crimps
- Fish tapes and poles
- Gloves (cut resistant)
- Hammer
- Handsaws and power saws (hacksaw, jab/rock saw)
- Headlamp
- Kneepads
- Label maker

As an electrician, you'll use a wide variety of hand and power tools. *fstop123/E+/Getty Images*

- Magnetic tray
- Measuring devices (tape, laser)
- Pipe reamer
- Pliers (channel lock/pump, diagonal, linesman's, long nose, crimps)
- Power drill and drill bits set
- Razor knife
- Receptacle tester
- Roto split
- Safety goggles
- Screwdrivers and nut drivers (full set, insulated, square tip, stubby, power)
- Thermal scanners
- Torpedo level
- Voltage tester
- Voltmeter
- Wire strippers
- Tool belt and toolbox

It's a good idea to start acquiring some of the most basic tools while you're still in high school—tell your friends and family who are wondering what to get you for your birthday, holidays, and graduation!

Different Types of Electricians

There are many different types of electricians. In the world of electricians, there are several ways of looking at the job.

Electricians Inside and Outside

One of the main conditions that separates different types of electricians is whether your work takes place indoors or outdoors. As the folks at State Continuing Education in Richardson, Texas, put it: "Choosing whether to become outside or inside electrical workers determines the overall direction of your career and will impact virtually everything you do as an electrician."[2]

INSIDE ELECTRICIANS

- Design, install, and maintain electrical systems that are inside buildings or other structures
- Provide buildings/structures with reliable electrical power
- May specialize in residential, commercial, or industrial work
- Usually work with lower voltages
- May work outdoors on aspects of projects that connect to indoor work
- Usually work regular hours
- Known as "wiremen" (although many are women)

OUTSIDE ELECTRICIANS

- Work outdoors on power lines that transmit and distribute electricity
- Ensure electricity moves from power plants to substations safely through high-voltage lines
- Usually work with higher voltages
- May have to work odd hours to respond to emergencies
- Known as "linemen" or "line workers"

High Voltage or Low Voltage?

Another division among types of electricians is whether they work with low-voltage electricity or high-voltage electricity.

HIGH-VOLTAGE ELECTRICIANS

- Maintain electrical systems using more than 600 volts
- Work on overhead and underground power lines, power plants, and other central electrical systems
- Work with potentially dangerous equipment
- Must know and follow all safety protocols
- May be on call beyond regular business hours
- May travel to various locations where maintenance or repairs are needed

LOW-VOLTAGE ELECTRICIANS

- Install, maintain, repair, and upgrade wiring and electrical systems in residential and commercial buildings
- Are sometimes known as voice/data/video electricians
- The National Electrical Code defines low-voltage systems as 49 volts or less
- States may have their own definitions of low voltage (in some places, low-voltage electricians are a different specialty from residential electricians)
- May specialize in particular systems such as cable and internet networks, CCTV, fiber optic networks, landline telephones, security systems, fire alarms, etcetera

Within these categories of electrician, there are many options. Let's talk first about all the different jobs you could do indoors (mostly) as an electrician.

Tip: No matter what kind of electrician you are, there's one thing you need to be extra careful about—*electricity!* Be sure to take all necessary precautions to protect yourself from shocks, burns, and other injuries.

Residential Electricians

This is the most common type of electrician job. Residential electricians work on all kinds of jobs that involve electricity in homes, condos, or apartments.

At the planning stage, residential electricians figure out where the wiring should go in a newly built structure or when adding power to an existing structure for new outlets, switches, ceiling fans, light fixtures, appliances, air conditioning systems, or whatever. To do this, they need to be able to read blueprints and technical diagrams and to know and follow relevant building codes. Residential electricians work closely with architects and building contractors. They test and inspect all the wiring and electrical equipment to ensure that everything is working well and safely before residents move in.

Residential electricians are also the ones who get the call when something goes wrong and needs to be repaired. Testing and inspecting is important here, too, to find out what the problem is, then come up with the best, safest, and most effective repair in a timely manner.

Residential electricians who work for construction companies usually can expect to have regular working hours, because most of their work is planned in advance and carried out on the job site during daylight hours. Sometimes weather or other unexpected events can change those plans, and electricians might have to put in some evening or weekend hours to keep the project on schedule. You might be working on your own or with others—either other electricians or workers from other building trades.

On the other hand, residential electricians who work for themselves or for small businesses might be called out at any time of the day or night to deal with an emergency. If you're self-employed, you may be able to set your own schedule to a certain extent.

Residential electricians mostly work indoors, but related projects or special fixtures like outdoor lighting on roofs or patios or installation of solar panels might require outdoor work. Expect to find yourself working in cramped conditions (attics, crawl spaces, basements), dirty places, or at heights. You'll frequently be working in places where the power is off (you might well have turned it off yourself!), so if the weather is very hot or very cold, you will be, too.

Commercial Electricians

Commercial electricians install electrical systems into larger commercial structures, such as office buildings or malls. These types of buildings require much more power than a home does. The commercial electrician reads the technical drawings and plans to understand how the wiring will go in, then installs, tests, inspects, and maintains all the wiring and electrical components being used. As a commercial electrician, you'll need to know all the local and national safety regulations relating to wiring and electricity in larger structures.

Commercial electricians usually work regular business hours (forty hours each week), but depending on the needs of the project (due to delays or changes), they might work overtime hours to get the job done.

Industrial Electricians

Large power plants or other large-scale manufacturing facilities employ industrial electricians to work on the heavy machinery and equipment that is required in these kinds of buildings. To work as an industrial electrician, you probably will need to be certified for this type of work while you are earning your apprentice or journey-level status.

Industrial electricians work in very large companies that may have multiple campuses or locations, so you may move from one job site to another. Expect to encounter heavy machinery and equipment and more electrical power in use than at a residential or commercial site.

Maintenance Electricians

Maintenance electricians work with large, critical electrical systems in places like plants and factories that rely on this power to operate. They make sure these large, critical electrical systems are safe and working efficiently.

As a maintenance electrician, you would need to understand and maintain the entire system of utility electronics and the power grid within the building or building complex, be able to repair those systems, routinely inspect all equipment, and repair or replace components proactively to prevent failures. In some jurisdictions, maintenance electricians might also be responsible for repair of programmable logic functions within a computerized electrical system.

MORE ELECTRICIAN SPECIALTIES

Electricians can also specialize in areas like these:

- Automotive
- Eco
- Electrical machine repairer and rewinder
- Electrotechnical panel builders
- Highway electrical systems
- Installation
- Instrumentation
- Integrated building systems (IBS)
- Marine
- Oil rig
- Sign
- Substation electricians

Specialized and Related Careers

There are several careers that are similar to that of the electrician. Some of these require different types of training or licensing. Some require more education.

Theater Electricians

Also called a theatrical electrician, the theater electrician is responsible for all aspects of lighting in a theatrical production (except for design) and for powering motors and other electrical items used during the show. That includes installing, pointing, and shaping a beam of light; connecting lighting instruments to power sources; and working directly with the lights to add gels, scrollers, or pattern effects to change the quality of the stage lighting.

There are many types of jobs within the role of theater electrician. For instance, the master electrician (ME) on a theater production supervises the other electricians and plans and implements cabling for lights and power distribution for the show. The ME (sometimes called the head or house electrician) is responsible for inventory, repair and maintenance, organizing and purchasing supplies, documenting and tracking the scenery circuitry, and

Working with electricity can be on large or small systems. *FlairImages/iStock/Getty Images*

solving problems that arise. The ME is also responsible for the health and safety of the other people on the electrical team specifically and for the whole cast and crew as regards electricity use for the show.

In the movie industry, the head of the electrical department is called a gaffer (or more recently, chief lighting technician or CLT). Gaffers need to manage all the electrical systems for the film shoot and to understand both electrical and natural lighting. Some other terms you may have seen in movie credits are "best boy" (the gaffer's assistant) and "key grip" (who is in charge of some kinds of equipment).

Don't miss the interview with theater electrician Jess Morton in chapter 3.

Electrical and Electronics Installers and Repairers

Electrical and electronics installers and repairers work on electrical equipment used in telecommunications, transportation, utilities, and other industries—everything from assembly line motors to sonar systems. These jobs can be very specialized, including the following:

- Commercial and industrial electrical and electronics equipment repairers who work with industrial controls, transmitters, and antennas
- Electric motor, power tool, and related repairers who work with such things as armature winders, generator mechanics, and electric golf cart repairers, and may specialize in installing, maintaining, and repairing electric motors, wiring, or switches
- Electrical and electronics installers and repairers who work on transportation equipment, mobile communication equipment, and surveillance systems
- Electronic equipment installers and repairers of motor vehicles who work with a range of complex electronic equipment, like digital audio and video players, navigation systems, and passive and active security systems
- Powerhouse, substation, and relay electrical and electronics repairers who work with the electrical equipment used in generating stations, substations, and in-service relays. They are sometimes called powerhouse electricians, relay technicians, or power transformer repairers

Because the work frequently involves electronic components of enclosed systems, the work environment is often inside a "clean room" where dust and other contaminants can't get into the components.

Most electrical and electronics installers and repairers work for manufacturers and utilities; others do repair and maintenance. This is usually a full-time (forty hours per week) job in the same location, although some travel to other locations is occasionally involved, depending on the project.

Electrical and electronics installers and repairers do not need to have the same kind of license as electricians. Certification is generally not required but a certificate from a professional organization can help when you're looking for a job. These professional organizations are also different from electricians. The Electronics Technicians Association International (ETA International) and the International Society of Certified Electronics Technicians (ISCET) are professional organizations for electrical and electronics installers and repairers. Both offer education and certification for a variety of specialties.

Electrical and electronics installers and repairers make a good income, ranging from averages of $82,700 for electrical and electronics repairers in powerhouse, substation, and relay environments to $37,380 for those installing and repairing electronic equipment in motor vehicles.

The Bureau of Labor Statistics (BLS) predicts the best job opportunities for those in this field will be for commercial and industrial equipment installers and repairers, whereas jobs for those who do aftermarket electronics installations in vehicles will probably decline.[3]

Line Workers

Line workers (sometimes still called "lineman" or "line installers") work on the power lines that transmit power from generation plants to local utilities, as well as to telecommunications (phone, fiber optic, etc.) cables. Line workers maintain the complex network of physical power lines and cables that provide us with electricity, landline telephone communication, cable television, and internet access. This is important work, even more so as the world becomes increasingly dependent on this kind of connectivity.

Within the general job description of "line worker," you can specialize by network or industry:

- Electrical power-line installers and repairers work on the electrical power grid. They are usually employed by local utilities and work with lower voltage distribution lines and sometimes traffic lights and streetlights. Most work for electric power generation, transmission, and distribution companies, as well as construction of power and communication line structures.[4]
- Telecommunications line installers and repairers work on lines and cables for network communications companies. Special skills are required for these specialized cables and equipment to troubleshoot problems and prevent downtime. Most work for telecommunications companies, with others working for utility system construction companies or building equipment contractors.[5]

You can also choose to specialize as either a line installer or a line repairer.

Line workers usually work a regular, full-time schedule. Depending on the project or if there is an emergency (such as a storm that brings down power lines), you may be called on to work long hours, evenings, and weekends.

Being a line worker is a physically demanding job that comes with serious hazards that could cause injuries. This makes knowing and following safety protocols and correctly using safety equipment extremely important. Even low-voltage electricity can be harmful, and high-voltage electricity will be worse.

Line workers may work at great heights reached by climbing poles and transmission towers or by being lifted in a truck-mounted bucket. This work can include installing aerial cables, sometimes over bodies of water. Line workers may also work below ground level in trenches, laying underground cable, conduit, or fiber optic lines. Safety training, insulated protective devices and tools, and fall protection are all essential to stay safe on the job as a line worker.

Wages for line workers are slightly higher than the average for electricians in general. According to the BLS, the median annual wage for power line installers and repairers in May 2019 was $72,500, with the low end at around $38,800 and the high end around $103,500. Telecommunication line installers and repairers are closer to the average electrician's wage, at a median annual income of $56,750, with the low end around $32,600 and the high end around $94,900.[6]

Electrical Contractors

An electrical contractor is a businessperson or company that specializes in designing, installing, and maintaining electrical systems in buildings during construction. Electrical contractors aren't necessarily electricians—they frequently are the ones hiring electricians (at all levels) as well as estimators, project supervisors, and other employees.

Electrical contractors are classified as follows:

- Outside (or line) contractors responsible for high-voltage power transmission and distribution lines
- Inside contractors responsible for all electrical and cabling design, installation, and maintenance for commercial, institutional, and residential buildings
- Integrated building systems (IBS) or voice/data/video contractors responsible for installing and integrating low-voltage installations (backup power, climate controls, wireless networks, energy-efficient lighting, telecommunications, fiber optics, security systems, etc.)

> One can prophesy with a Daniel's confidence that skilled electricians will settle the battles of the near future. But this is the least. In its effect upon war and peace, electricity offers still much greater and more wonderful possibilities.—Nikola Tesla[7]

Within an electrical contracting company, there are many roles for people with different skills and abilities. These might include the project manager or project supervisor, estimator, and journey-level or apprentice electricians.

In chapter 2, you'll find an interview with Sepp Herbert, an electrical contractor from Syracuse, New York.

Different Levels of Electricians

Like many tradespeople, electricians begin as apprentices, then earn their way up to journey level and, finally, master level, through a mix of classroom learning and on-the-job experience.

> **Tip:** Don't miss "Further Resources" at the end of this book! Look for the state-by-state list of licensing offices and departments with links to their websites.

Apprentice Electricians

Apprenticing is when you begin your career and your hands-on training as an electrician. During your apprenticeship, you'll work under the guidance and supervision of a master electrician and alongside journey-level electricians. If there was ever a perfect definition for "on-the-job training," this is it.

Rules vary by state, but in general you need a high school diploma before you can apply for an apprentice license. You work with a licensed electrician for a period of time specified by the state (usually 8,000 hours, which is around four years). You'll also be doing your classroom instruction during your apprenticeship, which usually amounts to between 1,000 and 2,000 hours. Check out

INDUSTRY-RECOGNIZED APPRENTICESHIP PROGRAMS

In March 2020, the U.S. Department of Labor (DOL) established a system for developing high-quality industry-recognized apprenticeship programs (IRAP). The program is intended to ensure that all apprenticeship programs meet high standards set by the DOL. To reach that goal, third parties called standards recognition entities (SRE) evaluate apprenticeship programs offered by trade and industry groups, corporations, nonprofit organizations, educational institutions, unions, and joint labor-management organizations to ensure they meet the standards.

An IRAP must provide participating apprentices with:

- Workplace-relevant knowledge
- Progressively advancing skills
- Paid work component
- Educational component

They must also result in an industry-recognized credential.[8]

"Further Resources" at the end of this book for where to turn for more information in your state, as well as for pre-apprenticeship programs that can help prepare you to be an apprentice.

Journey-Level Electricians

After completing your apprenticeship and passing the journey-level exam, you are considered to be a journey-level electrician, still often called "journeyman" or sometimes simply called a "licensed electrician." This means that you can work as an electrician without direct supervision. You might also be able to train apprentices yourself at this point.

The journey level is when many electricians decide to specialize in a particular career path. To maintain your journey-level license, you'll need to complete a state-specified number of continuing education credits and work a certain number of hours every year. Then you'll be able to take the exam that will qualify you as a master electrician.

Master Electricians

Master electricians have met the highest level of requirements in the profession. As a master electrician, you are at the top of your profession. You can supervise both apprentices and journey-level electricians.

Master electricians are eligible to work on more complex projects. Many master electricians start their own electrician or electrical contractor companies. Some states have several levels of licensing for master electricians, and some have separate license requirements for master electricians and for electrical contractors.

PRE-APPRENTICESHIP PROGRAMS

Pre-apprenticeship programs are available across the United States and Canada at local unions and International Brotherhood of Electrical Workers (IBEW)/National Electrical Contractors Association (NECA) training centers. The Electrical Training Alliance Pre-Apprenticeship Program (ETAP) offers introductory courses that last a few weeks or a few months (depending on the program) and give potential electricians the chance to learn more about the job, beef up their trades skills and knowledge, and find out more about signing up for an actual apprenticeship.

ETAP was started with a grant from the U.S. Department of Labor in 2015 to help meet the nation's economic and workforce needs by encouraging people to enter this skilled trade, especially those who historically have been underrepresented in the electrical industry.[9]

"These programs give people without any experience in the construction industry the preparation they need to succeed in our training programs," said Director of Civic and Community Engagement Tarn Goelling. "Apprentices who know what they're getting into are more successful than those who come in without that information. And these pre-apprenticeships are also an excellent recruiting tool for attracting a more diverse and local pool of candidates."[10]

To learn more about ERAP, go to: www.ibew.org/Civic-and-Community-Engagement/Pre-Apprenticeships.

To learn about requirements for ETAP, go to: https://nietc.org/pre-apprenticeship/.

In addition, different pre-apprenticeship programs can be found through state union or trade association chapters and high school trades programs.

The Pros and Cons of Being an Electrician

Being an electrician is a great career. You get to help people and solve problems, use your hands to make a real difference for customers, and earn a very good living, even without a four-year college degree. As with any job, there are advantages and disadvantages. Take a look at these lists of pros and cons and see what you think. Some of those "cons" might even belong in the "pros" column for you!

PROS

- **Full-time career**—as an electrician you will almost never lack for hours.
- **Job security**—electricians are in demand, and the need for electricians is growing.
- **A very well-paid trades job**—electricians in all areas make a good living.
- **Does not require a four-year college degree**—coursework through community or technical colleges plus an apprenticeship are a faster and less-expensive way to prepare yourself for a career.
- **Scholarships**—because of the big need for people to enter the trades, there are many scholarships to pay for the courses you do need.
- **On-the-job training**—electricians learn from other electricians, so you'll see the problems and solutions in real-life situations and get directions and feedback in the moment from others who know what they're doing.
- **Benefits**—electricians who work for an employer usually have good benefits, such as health, life, and disability insurance, and a retirement plan.
- **Union benefits**—many electricians are unionized, which helps ensure good wages and benefits, as well as safety regulations.
- **Opportunity for advancement**—depending on your specialty area, there are all kinds of ways to advance as an electrician. You might even end up being your own boss!
- Self-employed electricians can generally set their own schedules as well as their own rates.
- **You'll still have time for hobbies**—even with lots of work and those emergency calls, electricians still have time to spend with their families and to do the activities they enjoy.

CONS

- **Schedule**—because you never know when an electrical emergency may arise, many electricians must be prepared to work nights and weekends, regardless of your specialty.
- **Potential for injury**—there are hazards in any trades job, and even more when you're working with electricity. Be sure you are aware of the potential hazards on any job site. Using proper caution and protective gear and knowing and understanding the codes and safety procedures will minimize the chance of injury.

LEED-ING THE WAY TO A GREEN FUTURE

LEED stands for Leadership in Energy and Environmental Design. LEED is a global certification program that rates buildings on measures of sustainability. For a building project to obtain LEED certification, it must first meet the prerequisites. Credits are earned based on certain categories, and credits earn points. There are four certification levels based on the points system:

- Platinum (80+ points)
- Gold (60–79 points)
- Silver (50–59 points)
- Certified (40–49 points)

At a LEED-certified work site, electricians make sure that the work being done meets LEED standards for energy efficiency and pollution reduction and control. Back in 2009, there were about 19,000 LEED building projects around the world. By 2016, there were more than 80,000.

But the electricians' responsibilities go beyond the building's construction. They also need to be sure that the construction process meets the most current LEED requirements. That means things like requiring and maintaining a sustainable work site through things like alternative fuel sources and energy-efficient processes and using tools and products that reduce pollution and save energy.

- The LEED Green Associate credential shows that you have the most up-to-date knowledge and understanding of sustainable building practices and principles.

- The LEED AP with Specialty credential builds on the skills and knowledge of the LEED Green Associate.

Both credentials are earned by studying for and passing an exam. You maintain your credential with continuing education hours (fifteen for LEED Green Associate and thirty for LEED AP) and a biannual renewal fee.

You can learn more about LEED certification and associates from the U.S. Green Building Council at www.usgbc.org.

How Healthy Is the Job Market for Electricians?

The job market for all kinds of electricians is very healthy and getting healthier every day. Electricians of all kinds are in great demand.

What Are Job Prospects Like?

The BLS predicts that jobs for electricians will grow about 8 percent between 2019 and 2029. That's much faster than the average for all occupations. The BLS foresees more than 82,000 job openings for electricians *every year*. Electricians with multiple skills in different kinds of work (electronic systems repair, industrial component wiring, solar photovoltaic installation, etc.) will be the most sought-after candidates for jobs.[11]

As of May 2019, natural gas distribution companies paid the highest wages to electricians, whereas building equipment contractors employed the most electricians. The U.S. states with the highest number of employed electricians were California, Texas, New York, Florida, and Illinois, whereas the highest concentration of electrician jobs were found in Wyoming, North Dakota, Utah, Louisiana, and Idaho.[12]

Employment does fluctuate with the economy for those involved in building and construction, so you could experience occasional periods of unemployment if you work for a building contractor or similar company. Small businesses that respond to calls for emergencies or household repairs usually have steady work.

What Do Electricians Earn?

As an electrician, you can expect to earn a good, middle-class wage. Income will vary depending on your level (apprentice, journey level, master, or electrical contractor), as well as your location and whether you work for an employer or are self-employed.

The BLS notes that the average salary for electricians ranges from a low of around $33,000 to a high of about $97,000 annually, with an average of $56,000 per year. This is about 10 percent more than other construction trades workers.[13] The states where electricians earn the most (as of May 2019) are the District of Columbia, New York, Illinois, Hawaii, and Alaska. The cities with the highest average wages are San Francisco, California, Trenton, New Jersey, Mount Vernon, Washington, Lewiston, Idaho, and the greater New York City area.[14]

Summary

With so many options for different kinds of work, so much variety in what you'll do and who you'll meet and work with, and with so much need for more young people to enter the skilled trades, becoming an electrician is a wise choice. It's physically demanding and mentally challenging work, no doubt. There are important health and safety concerns that you need to be on top of, even more than in other skilled trades jobs. You'll need to keep up with your continuing education to maintain your license and rise through the ranks. The more education and experience you have, the more options will open in front of you.

As an electrician, you will be helping people and making the world a better place. You will have full-time, well-paid work without incurring a lot of student debt. Whenever you show up to work—whether in someone's home or business, at a construction site, a factory, a power plant, or anywhere else—you know you are making a difference and an important contribution!

In the next chapter, we'll talk about how to make your career plan so you can follow all the necessary steps to become an electrician!

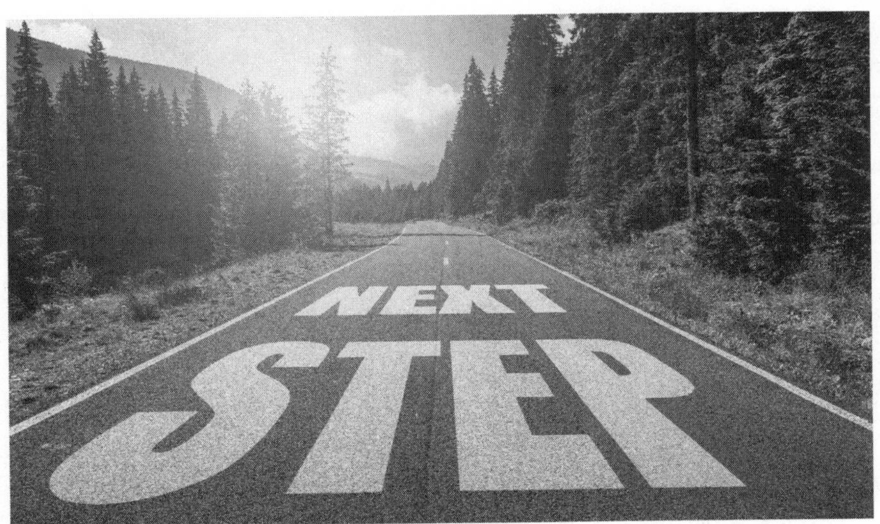

Plan your next step to reach your goal! *DaLiu/iStock/Getty Images*

JESSICA GRAY, APPRENTICE ELECTRICIAN

Jessica Gray. *Courtesy of Jessica Gray*

Jessica Gray is an apprentice electrician with Grayzer Electric in Austin, Texas. She has a bachelor's degree in marketing and communication from Tarleton State University, and prior to becoming an electrician, she did promotional work for Ford. Her now-husband Jeff (see his interview in chapter 4) invited her to work for Grayzer, so she started in an administrative/office role and helping out where she could. She then applied for her electrician's license at the apprentice level and began her career as an electrician.

How did you decide to become an electrician?

I got my license because I was tired of answering the phone and having people say, "Can I talk to an electrician?" It was my job to talk to people all day long about their electrical problems! I got my apprentice license so I could say, "You've got an electrician.

What can I help you with?" It also allows me to work in someone's home alongside Jeff or another electrician when they need me. So I do some residential electrical work and also help people with their problems from afar.

What is a typical day on your job?

On a typical day that I'm working on an electrical job, I would meet the lead electrician or ride with him to a customer's house. Generally, we check in with the customer when we're on the way there—a twenty- to thirty-minute heads-up. We go over what we have written down for the work order. If it's something new, we go over placement. If we're troubleshooting an issue, we go over that and do a walk-through with them. We get started with the work, pulling out materials, ladders, drop cloths, trying to keep everybody safe and healthy and clean. For an apprentice, the work is very hands-on. It might mean running back to the van to go get more material, or crawling in the attic to pull wire, or crawling underneath the house to check on some wiring—the very dirty parts of the job. If we have a job that's going to take all day, it's just a long day. For shorter jobs, we typically schedule about three jobs in a day.

What's the best part of being an electrician?

I enjoy being busy during the day. I don't like to have downtime, and there's no downtown with electrical work. I like working with my hands, physically doing something. I like always learning something new. No two days are ever the same for me—working with a new customer or on a new project. It's fun to learn these things that I might not have learned had I not become an electrician. One of the things we enjoy doing as electricians is doing the things homeowners aren't comfortable with and teaching them at the same time. Getting them to a level of comfort where they might try something themselves or feel comfortable calling us again next time. So they have the most information they need.

What's the most challenging part of being an electrician?

For me, the physical aspect of the electrical work. It's not at all uncommon for us to pull wire many, many feet. When we start using larger gauge wire, that can get pretty tough. I don't always have the same upper body strength as my male counterparts. Being an apprentice puts us in the least fun places. I don't want to meet a snake in an attic in the middle of a summer afternoon in Texas—I'm going to jump out of my skin!

What's the most surprising thing about being an electrician?

As someone who talks to the general public every day, it's surprising how little people understand about their electrical systems. The biggest part of what I do every day is teaching people about their electrical system: What does this component do? How does it affect the other things in the house? A lot of people are out of touch with how things work in their own home. It's not generally taught, and most people just don't know what's going on. We do a lot of teaching day to day, whether it's in the office or in someone's home. This is what to do if you have an issue. This is what to do before an issue arises. I grew up in the country, and you have to be able to fix things yourself. I could have become a master plumber, because you learn how to do these things yourself. Your parents would have to know what to do to teach it to you. Electricity is the one thing where you can't see it or hear it—but if you touch it, it's going to hurt.

The teaching information on the website is something we've been working really hard to get out there. It's not secret! Most of the electricity in a house, if you touched it, it would scare you and it would hurt, but it's not going to kill you. There's so much that homeowners can do inside the house. If you don't like the color of your outlets, here's how to replace them safely. We deal with a lot of people who are past their level of comfort, and that's fine, too. We're here for those people. We also do bigger projects that people can't take on for themselves. We do a lot of EV [electric vehicle] chargers—it's the green thing to do right now. We put in 220-volt circuits, 60 amps—that's a pretty dangerous circuit. That could actually kill somebody.

How did (or didn't) your education prepare you to be an electrician?

My college degree prepared me with the business side of owning an electrical company, specifically the communications area. I was an English minor. The marketing definitely helps us grow our "electrical community," and I put together our website. For the electrician part, it's important that the hands-on learning is very repetitious; it helps to replace outlets over and over and over to help you learn how to do that. To get an apprentice license in Texas, you pay the state a fee. We are required to do four hours of continuing education every year before the license renewal is due. The next license in Texas is the wireman's license, which allows electricians to work in someone's home by themselves while still working for a master electrician. Then you can test for your journeyman's license, which also lets you work in a commercial setting under a master electrician. I know there are some trade schools that allow you to have some class time one day a week or a couple of mornings a week, but the other days you're working for an electrician. Then you have the best of both worlds. Commercial and residential are very different in the way that things are wired, and people tend to be drawn to one or the other. It's like some people are good at algebra and some are good at geometry. There are people who can do both, but the majority of people are just naturally inclined more to one than the other.

Is being an electrician what you expected?

It is in some ways and it isn't in some ways. It is in knowing that you kind of start at the bottom of the ladder, and you're going to be doing the grunt work and paying your dues. I'm going to be supervised by someone who's been doing this a lot longer than I have, so it's my turn to do the grunt work. I'm surprised that I enjoy it as much as I do. I would not have expected that! I really enjoy doing different things every day. I just kind of thought that you graduate high school and you go to college, and after college you get a nice job in a high rise and you work toward the corner office, and that's what you're supposed to do. I did not take that route, obviously! I'm surprised to find that I do enjoy working with my hands more than I enjoy sitting in an office. From a business perspective, I do think it's easier to provide a more tangible service and get paid for it than to provide an intellectual service and get paid for it. For electricians and plumbers and HVAC technicians, we're providing a tangible service. You call us because something's not working, and when we leave, it is working. And I know that at the end of the day, I'm going to get paid for that. For some reason, society puts so much weight on "intellectual" work, when I would say it's the tangible services that really make our homes run the way they do.

What's next? Where do you see yourself going from here?

That's the million-dollar question. I really don't know. Grayzer is great. It's the way we pay our bills. It's the lifeline of our household. It's everything! But I also do really enjoy business for business's sake. I think I would enjoy doing something on the consulting end of things. Maybe help other electricians figure out how to start their own businesses. It's tough when you're trying to start your company in a market with a hundred other companies doing the same thing you are. It's not necessarily what we're trained to do as electricians. We're trained to go into somebody's house and fix what's broken, not necessarily to deal with vendors or fix those kinds of business problems. For the time being, I'll keep my apprentice license and think about taking my wireman's license test. And I'll keep on building our community and helping people fix their problems and add the fun things they want to their houses, like saunas and car chargers and that sort of thing!

Where do you see the career of electrician going from here?

I think there's a large portion of electrical work kind of turning toward solar and electric vehicles. There's so many robots to do things now—vacuum your floor, vacuum your pool, mow your grass. There's going to be a large push for electric motors, as well, as we become less dependent on fossil fuels and more dependent on creating our own energy and our own grids. I think there's a lot heading toward the photovoltaic—it's a growing section in the National Electrical Code (NEC). It's something that just wasn't there thirty years ago, but now every time the NEC is updated, that section is larger and more in depth. So having that knowledge of photovoltaic systems is going to be a big help.

What is your advice for a young person considering this career?

Ask questions! Ask all the questions! Never stop learning. It's going to be so much harder when you're out on your own. It's so much easier when you have a mentor to walk you through issues, because there are going to be issues. It can be hard to find a mentor, because you're either working for them or working for their competitor. But observation and questions—finding that mentor is going to propel you so much further than doing it on your own. When my husband started on his own, he was immediately hustling to find that first customer and build a clientele. It was really him bootstrapping it in the beginning. He didn't have a mentor to help him figure out what software he needed and that sort of thing. But he observed at every company he worked for and figured out what he did and didn't want to do, how he wanted to interact with customers and employees. And here we are nine years later.

For somebody who's applying for a job, as a business owner I look for three qualities in a new hire. I look for somebody who's humble enough to ask for help when it's needed and let us know when something is seriously wrong. I want somebody who's hungry—they want to work, which isn't that common any more. I want somebody who's going to keep asking for work and asking for advice on how to do this thing better and faster and easier. The third thing is somebody who's "people smart." A lot of what we do is reading between the lines of what customers are saying to figure out what they actually need.

Humble, hungry, and smart is what I look for in a candidate who's going to fit in well in our organization. But somebody who's got those qualities is going to make a great electrician on their own, to own their own company, if you're humble enough to ask a mentor for help, hungry enough to go out and hustle because your phone is not going to start ringing on day one, and "people smart" enough to know who is going to be your customer and who to say no to. We've got a friend who used to work for us, a phenomenal electrician, and now he's out on his own. He's doing a lot of remodel work, but his heart is really in service work. But he still is building his clientele to be able to do just the work he wants to do. It's back to paying your dues again, figuring out how to find your ideal client.

I think that the generation that's in high school now are figuring out that you don't have to go to college and I think that's great. I was told that was my only option: high school, college, job, get married, have kids—that's your life. Now people understand that they don't need to go into debt to have a career in life. They can just start in a career. I had no idea! I did love going to college. I think it set me up to get out of my tiny hometown, which is something I really needed to do. I think the trades are so great because you can get an education and get paid at the same time. As someone with very little experience, getting into a trade, you're going to work hard but you're getting paid. At the end of four years, you can test to become a journeyman electrician and easily double your salary. Whereas someone just getting out of college after four years is going to be in entry-level work. I was in college during the 2008 recession. Jeff was already an electrician and there weren't as many people doing things that weren't necessary, but there was no shortage of people needing trades. If someone's lights were out, they still needed to be fixed. There is no recession for the trades. They still are needed every single day.

2

Forming a Career Plan

Planning the Plan

Now that you've had an introduction to some of the many options in the electrician field, what do you next? Whether you want to go into one of these electrician careers, another skilled trade, or something completely different, you'll need to plan ahead.

So what goes into your plan?

1. First, you need to think about yourself—what you like and don't like, what you're good at and not so good at, and what feels like a comfortable fit for you.

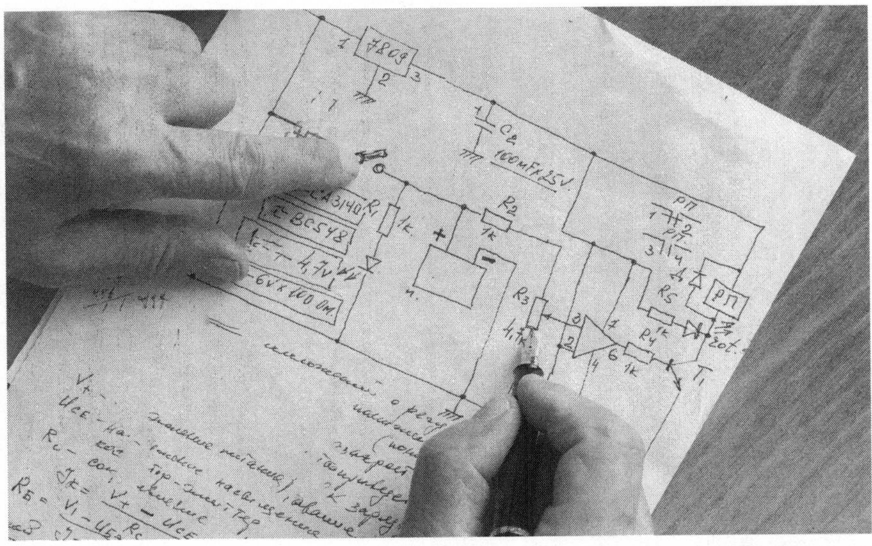

With a little planning, your career as an electrician can get started quickly and easily! *Mikhail Rudenko/iStock/Getty Images*

2. Next, you need to find some information—this can come from all kinds of sources, such as books, internet searches, and people you know or who work in your community. You can start with "Further Resources" at the end of this book.
3. Then, you need to know what you need to know: How do you get ready to pursue a career as an electrician? What can you do while you're still in high school?
4. What do you need to obtain your electrician's license? What kind of education will you need? What kind of training will you need? And how do you go about getting it?
5. Remember that the best plans are flexible.

> Just because something doesn't do what you planned it to do doesn't mean it's useless.—Thomas Edison[1]

In this chapter, you'll learn where to start and where to go from there. Let's start by making a few lists.

Figuring Yourself Out

Every good career plan begins with you. A good place to start is by thinking about your own qualities. What are *you* like? Where do *you* feel comfortable and where do *you* feel uncomfortable? Ask yourself the questions in the box titled "All about You" and then think about how your answers match up with a career as an electrician.

Remember, this list is for you. Be as honest as you can—tell yourself the truth, not what you think someone else would want the answer to be.

Once you've got a good list of your own interests, strengths, challenges, likes, and dislikes, you'll be in a good position to know what kind of career you want. For instance, if you like to talk to new people and you like to solve problems, you might make an excellent service and repair electrician. Or, if you are interested in moving up a career ladder, a commercial electrician job in a large business or institution or a career with an electrical contractor might provide more of those kinds of opportunities.

ALL ABOUT YOU

PERSONALITY TRAITS

- Are you introverted or extroverted?
- How do you react to stress—do you stay calm when others panic?
- Do you prefer people or technology and machinery?
- Are you respectful to others?
- Are you polite?
- How much money do you want to make—just enough or all of it?
- What does the word "success" mean to you?

INTERESTS

- Are you interested in how things work?
- Are you interested in solving problems?
- Are you interested in helping people?
- Are you interested in moving up a clear career ladder?
- Or would you like to move around from one kind of job to another?

LIKES AND DISLIKES

- Do you like to figure things out or to know ahead of time exactly what's coming up?
- Do you like working on your own or as part of a team?
- Do you like talking to people or do you prefer minimal interaction?
- Do you have a strong stomach or are you easily disgusted?
- Can you take direction from a boss or teacher, or do you want to decide for yourself how to do things?
- Do you like things to be the same or to change a lot?

STRENGTHS AND CHALLENGES

- What is something you accomplished that you're proud of?
- Are you naturally good at school or do you have to work harder at some subjects?

- Are you physically strong and active or not so much?
- Are you flexible and able to adapt to changes and new situations?
- Are you better at math than English?
- Are you better at computers or hands-on work?
- Can you manage your own time or do you do better when you're meeting a boss's or teacher's expectations?
- What, in your opinion, is your best trait?
- What, in your opinion, is your worst trait?

Now it's time to think about the characteristics of the different possible jobs you might do. Think about the location of the jobs and what kind of place you want to work. Would you rather go to the same place every day, where you'll see the same coworkers and work on a big system that you know every inch of? Do you want to focus on installing wiring in new buildings or homes? Or do you like the idea of the variety that comes from using your investigative skills to figure out how to help your customers?

For electricians, the type of education and training you need starts off the same way. But if you want to specialize, it's a good idea to plan for that in the courses you take and the kind of apprenticeship you do, as well as the kinds of jobs you apply for after you qualify.

Take a look at the questions in the box titled "About the Job" and consider the similarities and differences in electrician jobs.

ABOUT THE JOB

- What kind of work will you be doing?
- What kind of environment will you be working in?
- Will you have regular nine-to-five hours or will you be working evenings, weekends, and overtime?
- What kind of community would you be living in—city, suburb, or small town?
- Will you be able to live where you want? Or will you need to go where the job is?
- Will you work directly with customers?
- Will you have a boss or be a boss?

- How much education will you need?
- What are the licensing requirements in your state?
- Do you also need certification?
- Is there room for advancement?
- What does the job pay?
- What kind of benefits, if any, will the job provide?
- Will you join a union?
- Is there room to change jobs and try different things?

Finally, what does your gut say? Listen to the little voice in the back of your mind that says, "That's the one for me!" or "No way!" You already know what you'll like and what you'll be good at. A good fit is very important—more important than salary or many other considerations. So think it through with your head—but also listen to your heart.

Am I Right for a Career as an Electrician?

There are certain qualities that help make a successful electrician that go beyond the standard training and licensing requirements. Some are physical and some are personal. Some you can earn or build, and some you are born with. So what qualities does an electrician need?

- **Mechanical skills**—to know which tools to use for which job and how to use them.
- **Good vision**—you need to see well to read printed instructions and electrical diagrams. If you need adaptive equipment to read small print, be sure your employer knows to provide it.
- **Color vision**—electricians have to be able to distinguish between the many colors that are used to indicate the different functions of different wires.
- **Good hearing**—with or without adaptive equipment, you need to be able to hear well enough to distinguish changes in sound and pitch.
- **Visualization skills**—electricians have to be able to picture ideas and portray them graphically through drawings and plans (by hand and digitally).

- **Communication skills**—you have to be able to communicate clearly (verbally and in writing) with customers, coworkers, and supervisors. Communication involves both speaking and listening.
- **Physical strength, flexibility, and coordination**—you must be strong enough to lift and move heavy tools and materials, flexible enough to get into small or tricky spaces or climb to high locations, and coordinated enough to do so without falling or hurting yourself or others.
- **Troubleshooting and problem-solving skills**—electricians need to figure out what the problem is and then solve it. Your client can tell you the result of the problem ("The lights are out!") but you're the one who needs to figure out why and what to do about it!
- **Professionalism**—successful electricians are professional. That means showing up on time, giving fair estimates (for both time and price), being polite to everyone (customers, your boss, your coworkers, whomever you encounter). And, of course, doing the best job you possibly can.
- **Driver's license**—you'll need to get to and from different job sites, no matter what kind of electrician you are. For that, you'll need to be able to drive, and many employers require a driver's license. You also may be driving a company vehicle.

Where to Go for Help

There is so much information on the internet—about jobs and everything else—that it can be hard to separate the useful data from the noise. So let's take a look at how to find good information about electrician careers.

Start Where You Are

If you're in high school, you have a great resource when it comes to planning your future—your guidance counselor. It's your guidance counselor's job to give you *guidance* about your plans beyond graduation. If you're working on a GED at a community college or someplace similar, there is probably a career office that is there to help you. Take the initiative and walk in the door. Be sure to tell the counselor what you are interested in doing. *Speak up!* Remember, your counselor can't read your mind—tell them what you're thinking so they can give you appropriate advice. And don't stop there. . . .

Talk to Professionals in Your Community

There are professional electricians and electrical contractors in your town right now. Your family probably has a regular electrician that they call in an emergency. Maybe you have a relative or friend in the business. Ask them about their jobs, their hours, how they like it, what advice they have for someone considering the field, and if they can recommend someone else who can tell you more.

Of course, electricians are very busy people. But they know how much the field needs new people, so many of them will be more than happy to talk to you about the job. Some might even take you for a ride-along on a service call so that you can see the job in action.

If you want to get a closer look at a residential or commercial job site, you'll need to call the electrical contractor and ask if someone can show you around. You'll probably need to wear a hard hat and other protective gear while you're there.

Go to the Library

There are tons of books about the electrician career that you can look at. Some are aimed at the do-it-yourselfers who want to understand how their wiring and electricity work and learn a bit about fixing electrical problems. Others are for professional electricians. All of these will give you a good idea about the kinds of tools and equipment you need to be able to use and how it all fits together. You'll also find out important information like what kind of permits are needed for different types of jobs, when and who to call if problems arise, and which jobs should be left to the professionals.

So look in your school library and your town library. Go to Amazon and search for books about electricians, electricity, circuits, or wiring. If you find one you want to read and your library doesn't have it, they may be able to get it for you through interlibrary loan.

Google It!

Do your own research online. Sure, the internet is full of distracting memes and nonsense, but if you search carefully, you can find lots of information about every possible career. One great source of information is job postings. Take a look at the box titled "Hunt for a Job before You're Job Hunting."

Try some of these key-word strings to get started:

- So you want to be an electrician
- How to become an electrician
- Electrician license requirements
- "Residential electrician" jobs
- "Commercial electrician" jobs
- "Electrical contractor" jobs
- Technical college electrician program
- Community college electrician program
- Electrician scholarship
- Skilled trades scholarship
- How to be an electrician
- Jobs for electricians
- Electrician job requirements

HUNT FOR A JOB BEFORE YOU'RE JOB HUNTING

When companies want to hire new employees, they list job descriptions on job-hunting websites. These are a fantastic resource for you long before you're ready to actually apply for a job. You can read job descriptions for real jobs and see what qualifications and experience are needed for the kinds of job you're interested in. You can see what sort of tasks you'll be carrying out for different kinds of electrical jobs. You'll also get a good idea of the range of salaries and benefits that go with different levels of experience in the electrician trade.

Pay attention to the "required qualifications," of course, but also pay attention to the "desired qualifications"—these are the ones you don't *have* to have, but if you do have them, you'll have an edge over other potential applicants.

Here are a few job-hunting websites to get you started:

- www.monster.com
- www.indeed.com
- www.ziprecruiter.com
- www.glassdoor.com
- www.simplyhired.com

You can also find job listings on union and trade association websites. These will have great, useful job descriptions, too!

Making High School Count

If you are interested in becoming an electrician or going into any of the skilled trades, be sure you're making the most of your high school education.

Graduate

The most important thing that you can do to make your high school education count, of course, is to *graduate*. There are people who believe that if you're going into a hands-on job like being an electrician or one of the other skilled trades, finishing high school isn't all that important. Perhaps you know some older people—even relatives—who went into the trades instead of finishing high school. Maybe they're telling you that you can just apprentice and move up from there. This might have been true in some places a long time ago. But it's not true now.

In most states, you need a high school diploma or GED before you can enter an apprenticeship program and earn an electrician's license. Most employers list a high school diploma or GED as the first requirement on job postings. Most important, everything you learn in high school will come in handy as an electrician or in life—math, English, and business classes most of all. If you've already left high school without graduating, get your GED as soon as you can.

What Classes Should You Take?

Take the full range of general education courses in high school. You will definitely need a lot of math to do well as an electrician. English, communications, and business classes are also a useful choice. If your high school offers trades or vocational courses, especially anything to do with electricity, wiring, or circuits, take those classes!

Many high schools are starting to teach vocational courses again after a few decades without them. This is important! Well-paying trades jobs are going begging because there aren't enough trained people to fill them. One of the advantages of learning a skilled trade is that while you spend the same amount of time learning your trade as you would have spent earning a bachelor's degree, you are getting paid a surprisingly good income while you're still learning. That's a lot better than having a load of student debt at the end of the same time period.

Make the effort to study hard and do as well as you can in every class. You're learning more than just the subject matter. You're learning how to learn and how to tackle a project and see it through to the end. And *that* is a priceless skill that you can learn for free in high school.

> Vocational education used to be thought of in a very narrow way. It was considered simply an alternative track for high schoolers who weren't going on to college. Students often didn't graduate with a standard high school diploma. But career and technical education, as it's often called, has changed a lot in recent years.
>
> In many states, these programs no longer limit the opportunities after high school. In fact, a high-quality program may expand [your] options. Students in a good program should be able to graduate from high school with a standard diploma so they can go to college if they choose.—Kate Kelly[2]

Planning for Your Electrician's License

To work as an electrician, you have to have an electrician's license. In most cases, licensing electricians is handled by each state. You will have to meet your state's educational and work requirements and then pass a state exam to earn a license at each electrician level. Most states require continuing education hours and exams to maintain a journeyman or master electrician license.

There are a handful of states that do not license electricians at the state level. In these states, licensing and certification requirements are left up to each town or city. This can be confusing, so be sure you know what the rules are where you live and work. See "Further Resources" at the end of this book to find out who to contact in your state for more information.

For the purpose of this book, we'll just be talking about state requirements. If you live in a state that leaves licensing to municipalities, you can substitute the word "city" or "town" every time you read the word "state" below.

RECIPROCITY—WORKING ACROSS STATE LINES

Suppose you're licensed as an electrician in one state but want to work in another state. Maybe your spouse has been transferred or maybe you're helping out with a major emergency. Can you do that?

YES, IF . . .

. . . the state you are licensed in has a reciprocity agreement with the state you want to work in.

WHAT IS RECIPROCITY?

Reciprocity simply means that the states have an agreement that electricians (or other kinds of workers) who meet one state's standards also meet the other state's standards.

HOW DO I KNOW?

- The best way is to go to your state's licensing board website and check there.
- Another way is to look online at the NCCER Craft Licensing Map[3] on the National Center for Construction Education & Research website (www.nccer.org/news-research/reciprocity-map). Just click on your state and you'll see

a list of the states that have reciprocal agreements with that state. NCCER keeps this information as up to date as it can, but be sure to confirm with both states, as agreements can change.

Remember, states that don't license at the state level don't have reciprocity agreements with other states.

Educational Requirements for Electricians

We'll talk about the education path in detail in the next chapter. But first, let's look at what you need to know about educational requirements for electricians so you can include that when you're making your career plan.

Because each state's code is different, educational requirements for electricians vary quite a bit. You'll find different terminology and different licensing rules and regulations. It is *essential* that you check with your own state's licensing board first to find out what you need where you are. That said, most state's requirements are similar.

WHAT YOU'LL NEED

- A high school diploma and a completed apprenticeship are required to get your license as a journey-level electrician. We'll talk about apprenticeships in the next section, "Experience-Related Requirements for Electricians."
- State requirements differ, but you'll need a certain number of classroom hours of instruction either before or while you're doing your apprenticeship.
- You'll also need continuing education hours to move up to the journey level and then master electrician level and to pass the required exams.
- In most states, you'll need additional credit hours every one or two years and another exam to maintain those licenses.

Tip: Wondering why you need to take even more classes after you've already got an electrician's license? These continuing education courses are very important, as the code is complex and always changing. New techniques and new materials are also being introduced all the time. Without continuing education, you won't be able to keep up with the latest rules or the latest options.

Experience-Related Requirements for Electricians

To reach each level (apprentice, journey level, or master), you must demonstrate that you have the necessary experience. You'll start your hands-on learning in your classes in most cases, but your apprenticeship is when you really start doing the actual work.

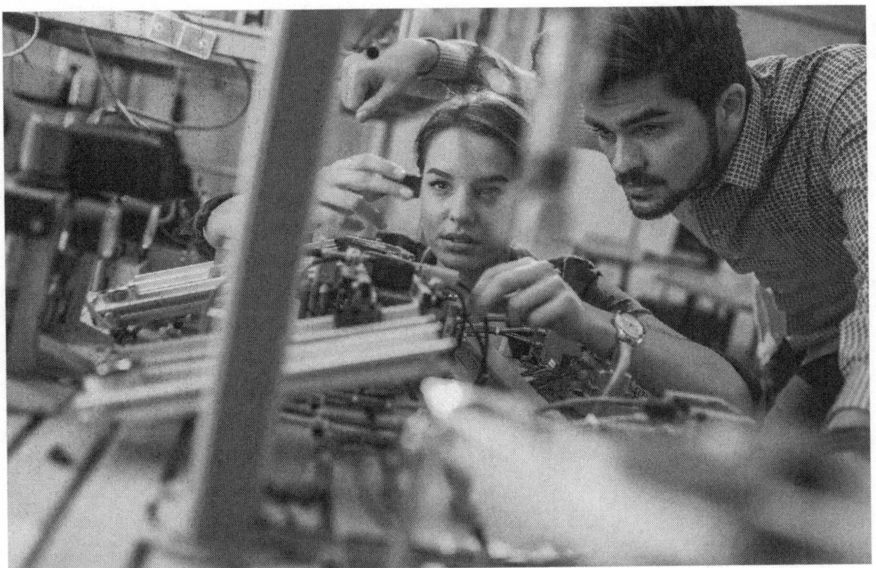

As an apprentice, you are learning by doing—with an expert teacher who is a professional in the field. *skynesher/E+/Getty Images*

APPRENTICE

To become an apprentice, you first need to find a master electrician who will take you on as your sponsor. You could be working with this person for four or five years, so it's important to find the right fit. Ask around in your area and see who you might want to work with. Look at online reviews of different electricians in your area. Talk to people who have apprenticed already. You can also search "electrician apprenticeships" in Google to find companies that are already looking for apprentices.

It's important to choose wisely, because the electrician you apprentice with is going to teach you all about the hands-on and customer-relations parts of the business. You want to learn from someone with excellent skills and a great reputation. You also want to work with someone who is a good teacher and who knows how to demonstrate the skills and how to properly correct you when you make a mistake.

Tip: Your mentor should show you how to do things the right way. It's your job to pay attention and make your best effort to do it right, too. Avoiding mistakes is a safety issue when you're working with electricity. But mistakes do happen. A good mentor understands that mistakes are part of learning and will have the patience to show you again and point out what you need to change. Your mentor should never belittle you or treat you like an idiot just because you made a mistake. Of course you'll make mistakes! You're there to learn.

The next step is to approach the master electrician you'd like to work with and ask if he or she will take you on as an apprentice. It's a good idea to have several good options on your list, because your first choice may not be able or willing to take you as an apprentice. They may already have as many apprentices as they can manage.

Requirements vary by state, so be sure to check with your state's labor board to be sure you understand the requirements that apply where you live and work.

Everyone currently working in the skilled trades is well aware of how many new people are needed. If the master electrician you approach doesn't take apprentices or doesn't want to take you (for whatever reason), that may not be someone you would want to spend years of your life working with anyway. Don't worry about it—just move on to the next master electrician on your list. You are needed!

An Apprenticeship Is a Learning Experience

Apprenticing is part of your education and training to become an electrician. For the hours you spend working under your master electrician to count, you need to be registered with your state (or town or city, depending on where you live). There is usually an online application form to fill out and possibly a background check.

Each state should provide information about what the requirements are, what sort of contract or articulation agreement needs to be signed, how many hours/years are required, and where to submit all that information so you get credit for it.

See "Further Resources" at the end of this book for a state-by-state list of the departments that oversee electricians throughout the United States.

An Apprenticeship Is Also a Job

Apprentices are considered employees. As an apprentice, you can expect to:

- Work full time—that is, a forty-hour workweek that will probably include evening and weekend shifts and emergencies
- Earn between $15 and $29 an hour depending on your employer, location, and union status
- Receive the same benefits as other employees (vacation and sick leave, medical and other insurance, retirement plan, etc.)

Some larger companies reimburse the cost of coursework; others cover the cost of equipment like tools, work boots, and a company cell phone.

The company's expectations will be along these lines:

- You will qualify to be an apprentice electrician according to your state's guidelines
- You are eighteen years or older
- You have a high school diploma or equivalent (GED)
- You have a valid driver's license with a good driving record
- You can pass a drug test and a background check
- You possess good communication skills
- You are a team player
- You have the ability to problem solve and prioritize
- You are flexible in terms of the hours you are available and the type of work you're willing to attempt or do
- You have a good attitude
- You are physically capable of doing the job
- You are willing to commit about five years to the apprenticeship

Some states require apprenticeship licenses, others don't. If your state requires an apprenticeship license, you will need to show that you have a sponsor (employer) or approved program. Learn more about state requirements in "Further Resources" at the end of this book.

There are a lot of details and differing state requirements for apprenticeship programs. If you look for an industry-recognized apprenticeship program (IRAP) (see chapter 1), you can be sure that your apprenticeship will meet the highest standards. The U.S. Department of Labor provides lots of information on its apprenticeship toolkit website at www.apprenticeship.gov.

JOURNEY LEVEL

Again, requirements vary by state. In general, to achieve journey-level (or journeyman) status, an electrician must complete an apprenticeship—however many years or hours meet state (or municipal) regulations—and pass an exam to get an electrician's license at the journey level.

To give you an idea of how varied these requirements can be, let's take a look at the requirements for journey-level electricians in three U.S. states.

Colorado Journeyman Electrician License Requirements

In the state of Colorado, electrician licenses are issued by the Electrical Board under the authority of the Colorado Department of Regulatory Agencies Division of Professions and Occupations. The Electrical Board notes that a journeyman cannot sign off on work for an electrical contracting company. Requirements to earn a journeyman electrician license in Colorado include the following:

- Eight thousand hours of experience earned in no less than four years as an apprentice, with half of those hours (4,000 hours) in commercial/industrial work[4]
- Two hundred eighty-eight hours of classroom education while registered as an apprentice
- Classroom hours must be documented with a transcript or similar statement
- Pass the journeyman licensing exam
- Renew every three years after completing twenty-four hours of continuing education in specific subjects[5]

Colorado also recognizes journeyman and master licenses from fourteen other states, as long as the license "is current, active, and in good standing and allows the individual to work as a journeyman electrician in the licensing state." Those with accepted reciprocal licenses don't have to take the written exam as long as they meet the requirements and pay the fee.[6]

Minnesota Journeyworker Electrician License Requirements

In Minnesota, to obtain a Class A Journeyworker Electrician's license, an applicant must:

- Have a minimum of forty-eight hours of work experience under a licensed master electrician, with specific numbers of hours in ten different types of jobs

- Apply for and successfully pass the exam
- Pay the application fee
- Renew every two years with sixteen hours of continuing education and a renewal fee[7]

South Dakota Journeyman Electrician License Requirements

The South Dakota Electrical Commission (a division of the South Dakota Department of Labor and Regulation) describes their requirements for a journey-level license[8] very simply:

- Four years (at least 8,000 hours) as an apprentice, working under an electrical contractor
- Pay the application and licensing fees
- Pass the journeyman exam
- To renew at the journey level requires sixteen continuing education hours, eight of those hours must be on the National Electric Code

South Dakota has reciprocity with sixteen other states for those who have earned their license in those states and held it for at least a year.

MASTER

Master electrician is the highest level of license. Having a master electrician's license means that you can employ journey-level and apprentice electricians, which means you have to know what they will need to know. The experience requirements for a master electrician vary by state, but in every case, you must have already met the requirements to become a licensed journey-level electrician. Beyond that, you must have a certain number of hours or years of experience under your belt, pay a fee, and pass a master electrician examination to receive this top-level designation.

Let's look at three more states and see how much experience a master electrician needs.

Wyoming Master Electrician License Requirements

In Wyoming, electrician licensing is handled by the Department of Fire Prevention and Electrical Safety. To qualify as a master electrician, you need to have:

- Eight years (16,000 hours) of work experience, of which 8,000 hours were completed with a journey-level license
- Five hundred seventy-six hours of electrically related classroom instruction
- Evidence of experience in planning, laying out, and following the National Electrical Code (NEC) under the direct supervision of a qualifying electrician or licensed electrical contractor in residential, commercial, and industrial settings
- Passed the master electrician exam
- Paid the license fee

Renewal is every three years with a fee and proof of sixteen hours of approved coursework, of which at least eight hours must cover the NEC.[9]

Vermont Master Electrician License Requirements

The Vermont Department of Public Safety, Division of Fire Safety, is in charge of electrician licenses in this New England state. Master electricians are responsible for "periodically inspecting the work of the journeyman licensees under their direction and performing a final inspection of the journeyman's completed installation."[10] To obtain a master electrician license, you need to:

- Provide proof of a valid Vermont Electrical Journeyman license for two years or proof of 16,000 hours of work experience documented by your previous employers
- Pay the application and exam fees
- Pass the examination[11]
- Renew every three years with proof of fifteen continuing education hours from state-approved institutions

As of 2020, the state of Vermont has reciprocity agreements with Maine and New Hampshire only.

Ohio Master Electrician Licensing Requirements

The state of Ohio is different from the others. There is no journey-level license there—you're either licensed or you're not. Electricians earn a state license as a commercial contractor for the Ohio Construction Industry Licensing Board (OCILB). Requirements are that you must:

- Be at least eighteen years of age
- Be a U.S. citizen or provide proof of legal alien status
- Have been a tradesperson in the type of licensed trade for which the application is filed for not less than five years immediately prior to the date the application is filed, or currently be a registered engineer in Ohio with three years of experience in the trade, or have other experience acceptable to the appropriate section of the board
- Never have been convicted of a disqualifying offense
- Pass the master electrician examination
- Carry a minimum of $500,000 contractor liability coverage
- Pay the applicable fees[12]

Renewal depends on continuing education credits and proof of continuing liability insurance coverage. For electrical license holders who have been tested and approved, there is reciprocity with six other states.

Networking

Networking is just a fancy word for getting to know people in a business context. It's about forming and maintaining good relationships. Networking is important in all businesses—including electricians—because business is built on relationships.

The old saying, "It's not *what* you know, it's *who* you know," is only partly accurate. To become a licensed electrician, it's very much about what you know! But who you know is also important.

What can networking do for you? You can . . .

- Meet other electricians and electrical contractors
- Find a master electrician to sponsor your apprenticeship
- Know who the best employers are in your area

- Learn important tips on best practices and new ways to do things
- Build your confidence as a professional
- Build your professional communication skills
- Make connections with other businesspeople and individuals in your community—they may send work your way, and you may want to send other kinds of work their way

> Networking may not come easily to you, and that's OK. But it's something you can and should get better at. It's worth the effort to become better connected. —Amanda E. Clark[13]

In her article "8 Steps to Better Networking" in *Plumbers Magazine*, Amanda E. Clark offered some useful tips to help anyone become better at networking at a business event. Yes, the article was in a magazine for plumbers, not electricians, but the advice applies to anyone in the skilled trades. Here's the short version:

1. Always be networking. Anytime you meet someone new, think of it as a potential opportunity. Have business cards ready.
2. Look beyond social media. A lot of the best connections you'll make happen face to face.
3. Be ready to market yourself. Have an "elevator pitch" ready to quickly tell people about you and your electrician business. What makes you and your company distinct?
4. Show up early. When you go to a conference, seminar, or meeting, try to get there a few minutes early so you have time to meet people, shake some hands, and learn some names.
5. Ask easy questions. Have some simple questions ready to use to break the ice and get a conversation going.
6. Share the things you're passionate about. Talk about the things you're interested in, but be sure you're not monopolizing the conversation.
7. Follow up on the contacts you make, via email or LinkedIn message, especially if you said you would do so. This may be the most critical part of the networking process.
8. Be pleasant. Don't forget to smile. Likability usually wins the day when all else fails. If people like you, they'll want to connect with you.

Getting along with other people is an essential path to success in any career. *Cineberg/iStock/Getty Images*

Whether you're looking for an apprenticeship, a recommendation to school or a potential client, referrals from other electricians, or to improve the reputation of your business, the best way is to know people, like people, and have them like you. You could meet your next big client or your new best friend. Who knows?

Summary

Now you know how to plan your plan! Everything you need to know is easily available to you. You just need to put out your hand and pick it up.

- First, be sure you know yourself.
- Next, figure out what you want out of your electrician career.
- Then, be sure you know what different kinds of electrician jobs are like.
- Learn what education and experience you need to achieve each level of an electrician's career and what your state or city requirements are.
- Finally, build your professional, communication, and networking skills by getting to know electricians, other skilled tradespeople, and folks in other walks of life.

Don't miss "Further Resources" at the end of this book! You'll find plenty of additional sources to help you figure out your plan.

In the next chapter, "Pursuing the Education Path," we'll look at what kind of educational options are available and answer the most important question—how do you pay for it? Don't worry! It's easier than you might think.

SEPP HERBERT, ELECTRICAL CONTRACTOR

Sepp Herbert. *Courtesy of A-W Electric*

Sepp Herbert is the owner of A-M Electric, Inc., a licensed and certified electrical and communication MBE/DBE contractor in Syracuse, New York. A-M Electric works with building contractors, educational and medical facilities, state agencies, airports, and the military on complex telecommunications and electronics installation, electrical inspections, and HVAC control wiring. Originally from Barbados, Sepp studied electrical engineering at Jackman Polytechnic College after training for eight years with his grandfather, who had an electrical company. A-M Electric employs administrators and office staff, as well as an estimator and project manager, who is a master electrician. Sepp is a member of the National Electrical Contractors Association (NECA).

How did you decide to become an electrical contractor?

I studied for two years at Syracuse University to study business management on scholarship. It was more like a boot camp course. I was working with the original owner of A-M Electric, and I realized that the business side of the electrical industry is also very important. So I was interested in electrics based on what I had learned from my granddad. I found that I had the ability to lead, and as I started doing more contracts and using my business skills, I decided I wanted to be a contractor. I wanted to accomplish goals based on being in the industry. There's no real glamour in being the boss. It's a lot of responsibility. You're responsible for your workers and their families.

What is a typical day on your job?

Getting up at 4:15 in the morning, working out, going over my things-to-do list. Work starts at 6:45 and the site opens at 7:00 a.m. You're dealing with your creditors, your foreman, your contract demands. You're dealing with the administrative side of the businesses, paying people, getting paid, guys with personal problems. With Covid, you're losing guys to COVID-19, but you still have the responsibility of paying them. It's a million things.

What's the best part of being an electrical contractor?

The end product. Seeing the product arriving from zero to a 100 percent, with all the trials and tribulations. It goes from the staff in the office to the people in the warehouse to the people in the fields to the owner, the architects, the engineers. Everyone is glad to see that. A job well done that comes in on time (if not always on budget)!

What's the most challenging part of being an electrical contractor?

Collecting money. Getting people to pay their bills. It's a trickling effect, because the person who has to pay you has to get it from somewhere else. The contractor has to front for sixty days before getting paid, so you're dealing with lines of credit, finance charges, late charges, paying distributors for product. Cash flow is one of the daunting things about being a contractor.

What's the most surprising thing about being an electrical contractor?

Losses. Economic loss. You're not going to always win. A lot of time, you're working hard to win, and then you get surprised by your loss. Sometimes jobs are so over budget that you don't make a profit on it, or sometimes you miss something about the scope of work that ends up costing you money because you didn't include it in the budget for the bid.

How did (or didn't) your education prepare you to be an electrical contractor?

It prepared me to understand the industry. The education from Syracuse University was very important, because it taught me the business administrative side. It gives me a broader education on how to read contracts and deal with the different scopes. It helped me understand the economic side, bookkeeping, the psychological side, understanding cash flow, payables and receivable. All three of them, because I had learned to do the practical things with my granddaddy. You have to learn, understand, manage, and implement. If you want to be in business, you have to have some kind of administrative education. You have to have the theoretical format before practical implementation.

Is being an electrical contractor what you expected?

It was a learning process for twenty-six years. I had no expectations at the start; I just knew I wanted to do electrical stuff. With the knowledge I have now, I don't know that I'd do it again! It's still a joy, though, and it brings a certain level of gratification, seeing the end product, dealing with people. Mechanics, academics, owners all see things from different perspectives. There's a whole heap of joint effort that makes it interesting. Dealing with your colleagues in the business and with families—you have so many people, different personalities, different family problems. It's interesting because it makes you think about how you're structuring your business to facilitate your goals. You go from the psychological side to structure your business to deal with issues that come up in families that affect the business. As a leader, it's important to pay attention to how the people on the team are surviving. This is how you become successful. I'm very conscious of my colleagues in the business, because if they're not happy, the business is going to suffer. If you're just thinking about an "I" position, you're going to lose. You can't do it all by yourself. The people are important.

What's next? Where do you see yourself going from here?

I would prefer the business to be sustainable. That's the healthiest and most interesting way for the business to be for me. That the cash flow is steady and the employees and their families are in a stable position. What makes it exciting and daring are the people around you who benefit. So after this, I would stop? Retire and enjoy life? I learned something about the word "retirement" from my dad. He said, "when I retire, I'm doing nothing." In the United States, people retire to go get another job to subsidize the shortfall in their income. So I don't see myself retiring, because what am I retiring from? And to do what? Your activity keeps you vibrant.

Where do you see the career of electrical contractor going from here?

I don't want to speculate too broadly, because I don't have the power to see the future. But because it's a local industry, you can't outsource it, so there will always be work as long as there are buildings and people. Technology changes, installation, different kinds of tools. As the industry incorporates new ideas and new technology, it will make the industry more viable. But there will be less physical demand; people may get less agile when the body's not working as much. Physically demanding doesn't have to mean exertion, but it's good for the body to move. I like some of the old school where there was more physical involvement. As we become more enlightened about different technology, it's obvious this will happen.

What is your advice for a young person considering this career?

It's a good trade, because I brought it [here] with me six hours by plane. It has a lot of dangerous implementations, because you can lose your life from a simple mistake, so you have to be serious and conscious, or you're going to get hurt. Stay in school, study math—math is very important in the electrical trade. There are very good benefits to being part of a union. You get legal courses, estimating courses, apprentice education that gives them the theoretical education as well as the practical, it gives them an edge over the ones who just learn on the job. You have to abide by the terms and conditions, but you also have freedom of speech and the ability to participate and effect change if you want to. I'm a member of NECA, the national organization for all electrical contractors. I'm a union contractor; I run a union shop; all of my workers except the office staff are members of the local union. So I can work anywhere in the country that has that affiliation. There's a joint partnership between NECA and the union IBEW [International Brotherhood of Electrical Workers]. For industries like mine, that affiliation is very important. For me as a businessowner, I know that I can go to the union and hire the right number of people who are all prepared to do what I need them to do. The union helps you access the pool of people that you need. The union is very good for business.

3

Pursuing the Education Path

It's probably become clear from the previous chapters that the path to becoming an electrician is very well-defined, with some variation depending on the type of electrician you plan to become and where you live. But how do you get from where you are to your goal of being an electrician? With guidebooks like these, plus your inventory of likes and dislikes, and the section "Making High School Count," both covered in chapter 2, you're in a better position than many of your peers to see what's possible for your future.

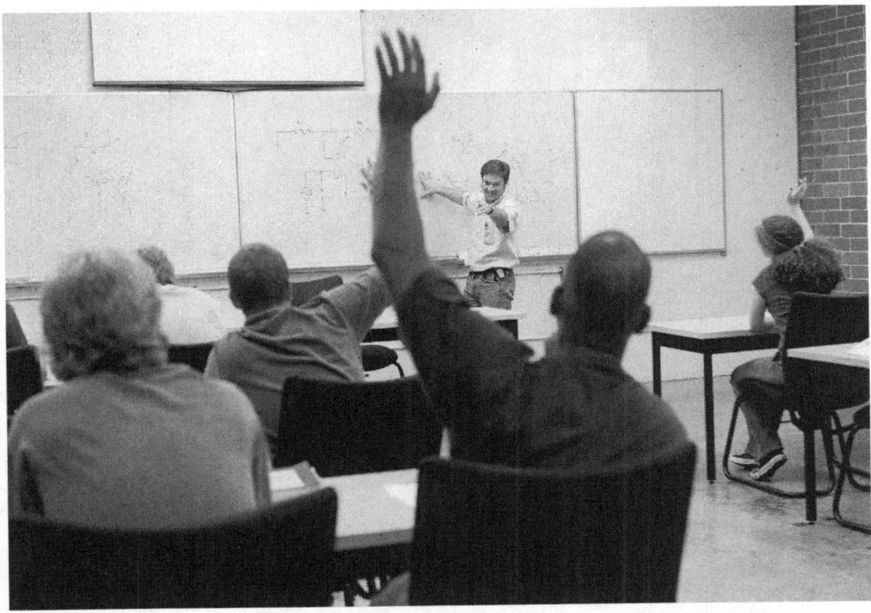

Education is the key to becoming and staying a licensed electrician. *lisafx/iStock/Getty Images*

In the skilled trades, your education happens in two different but equally important ways.

- **Coursework**: You'll need to take classes and exams throughout your career to reach each level as an electrician, maintain your license, and move up to master level. In some states, you need to have some classes under your belt before you start your apprenticeship. In others, you learn in class and on the job at the same time.
- **Apprenticeship**: You'll learn directly in a hands-on, learn-by-doing way from a master electrician (and the journey-level electricians who also work for that company) and get paid at the same time.

We covered apprenticeships in the previous chapters, so in this chapter, we'll focus on the in-school part of your training, along with licensing examinations and continuing education requirements.

Finding a School That Fits

There are many kinds of schools that offer the kinds of electrician courses that you'll need to pursue your electrician's license. So what do you need to consider?

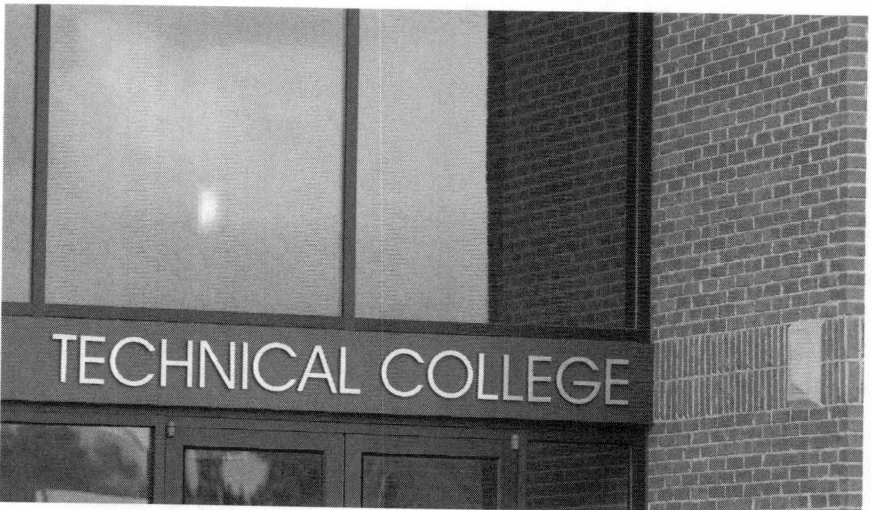

Technical and community colleges are an effective and low-cost way to get your education as an electrician. *sshepard/iStock/Getty Images*

Location

Where you need to be and where you want your school to be can be very different depending on where you live now, where you want to work, what kind of program you want to pursue, and what else is going on your life.

Start Where You Are

Always start from where you are. Sounds obvious, right? For people pursuing a skilled trade like becoming an electrician who want to live and work in (or near) their own hometown, the simplest and best route is to see what's available in your local area.

- What public community or technical college in your area offers electrician courses? Public community/technical colleges will meet your state's standards and are usually the best deal financially (see the section "What's It Going to Cost You?" later in this chapter).
- If you don't have access to a public community or technical college, is there an affordable private technical or trade school that meets your state's standards?

Different Places for Different Options

There are situations where you might want to go somewhere else to live and work, maybe because you think you'd like it better there, because you can earn more money there than in your current area, or because an opportunity has already come up there. For instance:

- If you live in Denton, Texas, but you have an apprenticeship offer from your aunt's friend's cousin in McAllen, Texas, you might want to find a school in McAllen where you can take classes while apprenticing.
- If your spouse is going to medical school in Boston and you currently live in Boise, Idaho, it might make sense to check out electrician programs in Massachusetts.

- If the nearest community college to you doesn't offer an electrician program, but there's a good one just over the border in the next state, you might want to look into moving there.
- You don't have to have a bachelor's degree to become an electrician, but what if you want one? You'll want to be sure that your electrician training program comes with an associate's degree or that credits easily transfer to a four-year college so you don't have to do the first two years again. It also might be more affordable to wait until you're working as an electrician and have some money in your pocket before you pursue a bachelor's degree. Of course, if you already have a bachelor's degree in some other field and want to become an electrician, there's nothing to stop you.

No matter where you choose for your electrician coursework, there are things you should pay attention to before enrolling.

Admissions Requirements

When you're looking at a college or technical training program, be sure you go to the admissions page of the website to find out the requirements. What's most likely follows here—but again, each college is different, so don't skip the websites!

Community College: Certificate or Associate's Degree Program

- High-school diploma or GED
- Free Application for Federal Student Aid (FAFSA—see the "Financial Aid" section later in this chapter)
- No SAT or ACT exam requirements ("open admissions")
- Probably a placement test (such as CollegeBoard's Accuplacer Placement Exam) to help you choose appropriate coursework
- Residency requirements may apply

Technical College

- Some have age requirements (sixteen, seventeen, or eighteen years of age)
- High school diploma or GED
- Placement test
- Some programs may require an entrance exam
- Good entrance exam scores can mean you skip the placement exam
- Residency requirements may apply

Academic Environment

Does the school offer the majors or certificate programs you want? Does it have the right level of degree program? What percent of classes are taught by professors and what percent are taught by adjunct instructors? Are adjunct instructors working professionals in the field? Does the school offer internships or help you find apprenticeships? Does the coursework match up with state standards and codes?

WHAT TO LOOK FOR IN AN ELECTRICIAN PROGRAM

How do you know what to look for in an associate's degree or training program to become an electrician? This quick list will give you an idea of what you should expect a good electrician training program to offer you.

- Experienced, highly skilled faculty who guide students through the learning process
- Many foundational courses covering different electrical systems, such as motor control systems, residential electricity, electrical construction, installation, and maintenance techniques
- Labs for hands-on learning on different types of electrical tech and machinery
- Elective courses that can lead to specialization

Financial Aid Options

This is something you have to look at carefully—see the "Financial Aid" section below. Sometimes, employers pay the cost of coursework taken by their apprentices. If you get a deal like that, you need not worry about financial aid. But not every employer can or will make that offer.

Don't worry if you need financial aid! There are lots of scholarships for people who want to learn a skilled trade. Does your community or technical college provide access to scholarships, grants, work-study jobs, or other opportunities? Is the cost of school a major part of your decision?

Support Services

Support services include things like academic counseling, career counseling, health and wellness, residence services, the financial aid office, information technology (IT) support, commuter services, and services for students who are disabled, or who have families, or who are lesbian, gay, bisexual, or transgender. Before you choose a school, look through the website and be sure it provides the services you need.

Clubs/Activities/Social Life

Most colleges have clubs and other social activities on campus, whether the student population is mostly residents or mostly commuters. Look for clubs related to the trades you're interested in, as well as clubs and activities that meet your other interests. College campuses have all kinds of things going on all the time, for students and for the local community. Don't miss out!

Specialized Programs

Does the school or program have any programs that meet your specialized needs? For instance, some institutions have programs specifically for veterans. Some address learning disabilities. Do they provide mental health counseling services?

Housing Options

Will you need on-campus housing? Many community and technical colleges expect most of their students to be commuters, but some provide on-campus housing. What kind of housing options do you want and need? Does the college provide dorms? How many students will share a room? Are there on-campus apartments? Is there help with finding off-campus housing like apartments or rooms for rent?

Transportation

If you live off campus, how will you get to school? Is there a bus system—campus or municipal? Is there a ride-share program? Could you ride a bicycle? Will you need to have access to a car? If you do, is there enough parking? Is there an on-campus shuttle bus service that can get you around quickly if you're attending a large campus?

Student Body

What will the other students be like? What's the ratio of males to females? Is there enough diversity? Are most of the students residents or commuters? Part time or full time? Who will you meet?

Tip: Be sure you aren't paying too much! Watch out for education scams that are just out to sell you expensive student loans. If you work through your local community or technical college and follow up on all the available scholarships for people going into the skilled trades, you shouldn't need to take out a lot of student loans.

What Degree Will You Earn?

In most states, you can earn an electrician's license without a specific degree or any college degree at all. As long as you take the right courses, complete your

Classroom education enables you to learn the right things in the right order. *iStock/Getty Images*

apprenticeship, and pass the exam, you can earn your electrician's license. But having an associate's degree can help you be more competitive in the job hunt. And if you decide you want a bachelor's degree (perhaps in business or electrical engineering) later on, you'll already be halfway there.

So how do you choose the program that's right for you? It depends on several things:

- What are your goals?
- What kinds of programs are available where you live?
- If you want a different kind of program, can you travel or move where that program is offered?

What Are the Educational Options?

Most community and technical colleges offer electrician coursework as part of a structured program. These programs present the information you'll need to know sequentially so that what you learn in one class helps you with what you'll be learning in later classes. That's one of the big advantages to taking classes! Community and technical college electrician programs will be designed to meet the standards of the state where they're located, as well.

Associate's Degree

Every electrician training program is unique, but they also have a lot in common. To get an idea of what you might find in an associate's degree program, let's take a look at what's offered in two different states: New Hampshire and Arizona.

Example 1: Manchester Community College, New Hampshire

Manchester Community College is located in the largest city in New Hampshire. Its associate in applied science (AAS) degree in electrical technology takes two years to complete. In New Hampshire, an associate's degree like this one can be used toward your electrician's license, along with 8,000 hours of field experience under a licensed journey-level or master electrician. The degree can be used in place of 600 hours of nondegree coursework (with an emphasis on electrical safety) or ten or more years of experience.

Admissions requirements include the following:

- College-level reading skills
- Placement in a specific math course: numerical algebra and trigonometry
- An interview with the program coordinator

For those who aren't seeking an associate's degree, Manchester Community College also offers a thirty-nine credit electrical technology certificate and a twenty-four credit electrical lineworker certificate.

Table 3.1. Manchester Community College AAS Electrical Technology Degree (67 Credits)

		Course Credits	*Total Semester Credits*
Year 1			
Semester 1	Electrical Fundamentals I	4	
	Electrical Fundamentals II	4	
	Numerical Algebra and Trigonometry	3	
	Microsoft Computer Applications I	3	
	MCC Essentials	1	15
Semester 2	Power, Transformers, and Rotating Machinery	4	
	Residential, Commercial, and Industrial Wiring	4	
	Intermediate Algebra or Intermediate Algebra—Corequisite	4	
	College Composition I (maybe with Corequisite)	4	
	Business Elective	3	19
Year 2			
Semester 1	Electrical and Electronic Motor Controls	4	
	Commercial and Low-Voltage Building Systems	4	
	College Algebra with Trigonometry	4	
	Professional Communication	3	
	Social Science Elective	3	18
Semester 2	Advanced Controls, Digital Fundamentals, PLC Basics	4	
	Renewable and Alternative Energy Systems	4	
	College Physics I	4	
	Foreign Language/Humanities/Fine Arts Elective	3	15
	TOTAL CREDITS		**67**

Example 2: GateWay Community College, Phoenix, Arizona

AAS in construction trades: Electricity is a degree program for apprentices and journey-level electricians that provides "a broadened educational background and leadership skills so that students completing the associate degree program may be better equipped to enter supervisory and managerial positions."[2] Notice how the semesters and courses are arranged differently from the previous example (see table 3.2). This program takes more semesters because each semester has fewer courses—something that could be helpful for people also working in an apprenticeship.

Table 3.2. GateWay Community College AAS Electrical Technology Degree (Minimum of 88+ Credits)

Semester	*Course*	*Credits*
1	Construction Electricity I	6
2	Introduction to National Electrical Code (NEC)	3
3	Construction Electricity II	6
	English 101 First-Year Composition or English 107 First-Year Composition for English as a Second Language	3
4	Construction Electricity III	6
	English 102 First-Year Composition or English 108 First-Year Composition for English as a Second Language	3
	Technical and Professional Writing	3
5	National Electrical Code I	3
6	Construction Electricity IV	6
	College Critical Reading and Critical Thinking (or equivalent by exam)	3
7	Advanced Construction Electricity I	6
	Intermediate Algebra 120, 121, 122, or equivalent	3–5
8	National Electrical Code II	3
	Social and Behavioral Sciences general education course	3
9	Advanced Construction Electricity II	6
	Any one of three approved communications courses	3
10	Advanced Construction Electricity III	6
	Humanities/Fine Arts general education course	3
11	National Electrical Code III	3
12	Advanced Construction Electricity IV	6
	Natural Sciences general education course	4
	Restricted electives courses	0–8
	TOTAL CREDITS	**88+**

To be admitted to this program, students must first register with the Arizona State Apprenticeship Office. The program has a mix of general education courses, required courses, and restricted electives (i.e., a choice from among a set group of courses relating to the major).

Bachelor's Degrees

You don't need a bachelor's degree to have a long and successful career as an electrician. However, whether you're just starting out, have finished an associate's degree, or have been working as an electrician for a while, you might want to consider a bachelor's degree. Having a bachelor's degree means that you have put in the effort to learn even more about your field and are better prepared to work at a higher level. Earning a bachelor's degree is not just about the subject matter in your courses. It includes developing your critical thinking skills, your analytical skills, your problem-solving skills, as well as giving you a broader view of the world and everything in it.

For an electrician, a bachelor's degree can be useful if you want to build on your skills and knowledge to do the following:

- Move up into management, estimating, or other administrative areas in your company
- Become an electrical engineer
- Become an electrical contractor
- Improve your own electrician business

There are many bachelor's degrees available depending on where you want to go. Some of the options you might find are discussed next.

What to Look for in a Bachelor's Degree Program

Choosing a bachelor's degree program is a lot like choosing an associate's degree program. You have to look for the following:

- The right academic program (does it offer the degree you want?)
- The right fit (in terms of all those aspects we talked about earlier in the chapter—things like location, support services, housing, financial aid, transportation, and so forth)
- Cost (including tuition rates and available financial aid in the form of scholarships, grants, loans, and work-study programs)

Don't Leave Credits on the Table—Transferring

If you have already completed an associate's degree, you should look for a program that will accept that degree or those two years of college courses as transfer credits. By transferring the credits you have already earned, you can cut your time toward a bachelor's degree in half. That lets you focus on only the coursework you need for your major and the electives that you most want to take.

Different institutions have different rules about what transfer credits they accept as well as time limits on how long ago those courses were completed. If you want to transfer credits into a bachelor's degree program, be sure to talk to the admissions office to find out what you can and can't transfer, as well as the right way to do it.

Electrician's License Exams

At each stage of an electrician's career, there are licensing exams through the state that you must pass to earn and then keep your license to work as an electrician at a particular level.

Tip: Don't miss "Further Resources" at the end of this book! Look for the state-by-state list of licensing offices and departments with links to their websites.

Apprentice Electrician License

As of 2020, only three states (Alaska, Iowa, and Maine) and the District of Columbia require a license at the apprentice electrician level. This type of license generally also applies to electrician's assistants who are not doing an apprenticeship.

Most states require would-be apprentices to fill out an application signed by the employer they'll be working under—essentially a contract among the apprentice, the master electrician, and the state where the apprentice will complete the training and work the program for the required amount of time. Be sure that you understand the rules in your state and that you follow them to the letter!

Journey-level Electrician's License

Once again, each state is different. In some states, you can do electrical jobs on your own as a journey-level electrician. You apply for this license after completing your state's requirements for an apprentice electrician and passing an exam. Here's a quick sample of how much state requirements can differ:

- The state of Alabama specifies no less than four years of experience in electrical wiring, apparatus, or equipment, light, heat, or power. However, some electrical education in electrical curriculum can substitute for one of those four years of experience.
- In Delaware, you must have at least three years of practical experience or two years of schooling plus one year of practical experience and pass a written exam to reach the journey-level license. Delaware also offers two other mid-level licenses:

  1. Limited electricians (limited to air conditioning, oil burners, signs, elevators, and overhead and underground primary distribution systems, etc.)
  2. Limited special electricians (limited to residential wiring)

- In Maryland, journey-level electricians are licensed at the county level rather than by the state.
- In North Carolina, the state doesn't mandate licensing requirements for journey-level electricians, and only some of the municipalities have their own requirements.
- Rhode Island has five types of journey-level electrician licenses: journeyperson electrician, electrical sign installer, fire alarm installer, oil burner person, and lightning protection installer.

Master Electrician's License

Each state has specific rules and regulations, but, in general, to obtain a master electrician's license, you need to have a certain number of years (usually two, or about 4,000 hours) as a journey-level electrician. Then you have to take and pass the master electrician's exam.

As usual, things vary a lot by state. For instance, in some states (such as Louisiana, Nevada, and New Jersey), a master electrician is essentially the same thing as an electrical contractor. In other states (such as Hawaii, Idaho, and North Dakota), those are two different things with different licensing requirements. In Oregon, a master electrician's license is issued through the Building Codes Agency, whereas an electrical contractor's license is issued by the Construction Contractors Board.

Continuing Education

Continuing education is how skilled tradespeople keep their skills up to date and learn the latest technical, safety, and legal requirements for their fields. Continuing education is also required to maintain your electrician license at any level.

Each state has its own requirements for how many continuing education credits you need to earn within a certain period of time. This might vary by professional level. Be sure you know what your state's requirements are to keep up your licensing or certification requirements. For example:

- In Utah, the Division of Occupational and Professional Licenses requires twelve core hours and four professional hours of continuing education to renew an electrician's license.
- In Texas, licenses at all levels are valid for one year. You must complete four hours of continuing education during that year to renew your license. These courses must address the National Electrical Code, Texas Electrician Law, Texas Electrician Administrative Rules, and National Fire Protection Association electrical safety rules.
- In Kentucky, at least six hours of continuing education each year is required to renew your license.

What's It Going to Cost You?

There are a lot of other factors that affect the cost of your education and training to become an electrician. Are you going to a community college,

Table 3.3. Annual Costs—Undergraduate College/University

	Public			*Private (Nonprofit)*
2019–2020	*Two-Year In-District*	*Four-Year In-State*	*Four-Year Out-of-State*	*Four-Year*
Tuition and Fees	$3,730	$10,440	$26,820	$36,880
Room and Board	$8,990	$11,510	$11,510	$12,990
Combined	$12,720	$21,950	$38,330	$49,290

Source: College Board Research Department https://research.collegeboard.org/trends/college-pricing.

technical college, or other trade school? How much financial aid are you eligible for in terms of scholarships or grants? How much will you be expected to borrow in student loans?

The information in table 3.3 is available on the College Board website (www.collegeboard.org) and represents average annual costs for full-time students during the 2019–2020 academic year. (It's worth noting that these numbers represent an average increase of 2.7 percent over 2018–2019 costs before adjusting for inflation). Costs shown are for one year.

That's a lot of money! *However*, these are averages. In general, tuition and other costs for college tend to increase about 3 percent every year, so take that into consideration when planning for the year that you'll be going to school. You'll need to look closely at the costs of the schools you're considering—they could be quite different from these.

But don't worry! There are all kinds of ways to get those costs down!

Financial Aid

It really can pay off to put some time and effort into discovering what financial aid you qualify for. Reach out to the financial aid office at the school you want to attend. It can offer a lot of information about what may be available.

Financial aid can come from many sources. The kind of awards you're eligible for depend on a lot of things, such as:

- Academic performance in high school
- Financial need
- Program/field
- Type of college

NOT ALL FINANCIAL AID IS CREATED EQUAL

Educational institutions tend to define financial aid as any scholarship, grant, loan, or paid employment that assists students to pay their college expenses. Notice that "financial aid" includes both money you *have to pay back* and money you *don't have to pay back*. That's a big difference!

Does Not Have to Be Repaid:

- Scholarships
- Grants
- Work-Study

Has to Be Repaid *with Interest*:

- Federal government loans
- Private loans
- Institutional loans

Tuition Benefits

Before you apply for scholarships or loans, first find out if you are eligible for money for classes from outside sources.

Employer Tuition Benefit

Because the skilled trades desperately need so many new people, some employers are willing to pay some or all of the cost of coursework for their apprentices. This isn't something every employer can afford, but if you are trying to choose among several electrician apprenticeship options, a course tuition benefit can be an important factor in helping you decide. Even if the company can contribute only part of the cost, every bit helps.

Union Tuition Benefit

Are you already a union member? As with employers, benefits vary from union to union and from state to state. But unions provide important benefits to their members, and education is often one of them.

Scholarships

> While it seems easy enough to simply start searching online for scholarships, if you approach it with a more refined touch, your results will substantially increase. The key is to not find all scholarships available, but to quickly go through them to find the scholarships available to you, as the unique individual you are.—GoCollege.com[5]

Scholarships are financial awards that are usually offered on the basis of academic merit, membership in a particular organization, or for people going into a particular field—like electricians or other skilled trades. Scholarships also can be available to students who meet certain criteria (e.g., athletes) or who are underrepresented in a particular field or major (e.g., women or members of a minority group). Some scholarships go toward tuition; others are for things like textbooks and school supplies.

Scholarships usually pay part (not all) of tuition—it is very rare to receive a full-tuition scholarship, though it does happen. Scholarships do not have to be paid back. Scholarships can be local, regional, statewide, or national in scope.

There are also scholarships specifically for community college students, including those who want to transfer to a bachelor's degree program later or those who are studying a particular subject. Some are offered by professional associations, some by nonprofit organizations, and some by the community colleges themselves.

SCHOLARSHIPS FOR THE SKILLED TRADES

Many scholarships exist to help encourage more people to enter the skilled trades. There are scholarships sponsored by states, by private foundations, by professional organizations, and more. Here are just a few scholarships for people who want to be electricians:

- Frank J. Blau Jr. Scholarship
- Jill Reed Women in Trades Scholarship
- Jim "Buddha" Potts Memorial Veterans—A Troops to Trades Scholarship
- John J. MacGregor Scholarship
- A. O. Smith Professional Contractors Association
- Work Ethic Scholarship Program from the Mike Rowe Works Foundation
- Horatio Alger Career and Technical Scholarship
- AGC Undergraduate Scholarship

There are many others. Some are for specific schools, for students living in certain areas, or for people who went to a particular high school. Go to "Further Resources" at the end of this book for links to websites with much, much more information on how you can fund your education. This is free money for people like you! Don't miss out!

Scholarships are free money to pay for your education. *Kuzma/iStock/Getty Images*

Grants

Grants are similar to scholarships. Most tuition grants are awarded based on financial need, but some are restricted to students in particular sports, academic fields, demographic groups, or with special talents. Grants do not have to be paid back.

Some grants come through federal or state agencies, such as the Pell Grant, SMART Grants, and Federal Supplemental Education Opportunity Grant (FSEOG). You'll need to fill out the FAFSA form (see the "Loans" section below). Learn more about those at studentaid.ed.gov/types/grants-scholarships.

Grants also are awarded from private organizations or from the college itself. For instance, some private colleges or universities have enough financial resources that they can "meet 100 percent of proven financial need." That doesn't mean a free ride, but it usually means some grant money to cover the gap between what the financial aid office believes you can afford and the amount covered by scholarships and federal loans (more on federal loans below).

Work-Study

The federal work-study program provides money that college students can earn through part-time jobs. Work-study is a need-based program, so you'll need to find out if you are eligible for it. Some students are not eligible at first but become eligible later in their college career. Most jobs are on campus, some relate to your field, but others—like working in the library—could be more general.

Some colleges and universities don't participate in the work-study program, so check with the financial aid office to see if it's available and if you're eligible for it. It's good to apply early so that you have a better chance of getting the job you want most.

Since work-study is earned money (you work a job and get paid for it), this money does not need to be paid back. To learn more, check out studentaid.ed.gov/sa/types/work-study.

Loans

There is almost always a gap between tuition and the amount of money you receive from a school in scholarships and grants. That gap is filled by student loans. Student loans have to be repaid. Interest varies depending on the type of loan. Be sure you understand how much interest you will be charged, when the interest starts to accumulate, and when you must start paying the loan back. Usually, repayment starts when you graduate or after a six-month grace period.

FEDERAL LOANS

Federal student loans are issued by the U.S. government. They have lower interest rates and better repayment terms than other loans. You don't need anyone to cosign for your debt. If the loan is subsidized, the federal government pays the interest until you graduate. If it's unsubsidized, interest starts to accrue as soon as you accept the loan. That can amount to a very big difference in how much you pay for your education by the time the loan is paid off.

The most common federal student loan is the low-interest Federal Stafford Loan. Depending on household income, a student's Stafford loan might be subsidized or unsubsidized.

Most schools will require you to fill out the FAFSA when you apply for financial aid. FAFSA stands for Free Application for Federal Student Aid. Note that it doesn't say "free student aid"; it says "free *application*." That means it does not cost anything to *apply* for federal student aid. You may get "offers" to submit the FAFSA for you for a fee—this is a scam. Don't do it.

PRIVATE LOANS

Chances are, federal student loans will not completely fill the gap between your tuition bill and any scholarships or grants you receive. Private student loans are issued by a bank or other financial institution. Rates of interest are generally higher than for federal loans, so be careful not to borrow more than you need. Eligibility criteria for private loans are based on your (and your cosigner's) credit history.

Don't simply take the first loan you find. Do some research; compare interest rates and terms. Is the interest variable or fixed? Is there a cap on the variable interest? Is the company reputable? What are the repayment requirements?

INSTITUTIONAL LOANS

Many educational institutions make their own loans using funds provided by donors such as alumni, corporations, and foundations, as well as from repayments made by prior college loan borrowers. Every college has its own rules, terms, eligibility, and rates. Interest may be lower than private student loans, and deferment options may be better, as well.

Learn more about all kinds of financial aid through the College Board website at bigfuture.collegeboard.org/pay-for-college.

FINANCIAL AID TIPS

- Some colleges/universities offer tuition discounts to encourage students to attend—so tuition costs could be lower than they first appear.
- Apply for financial aid during your senior year of high school. The sooner you apply, the better your chances. Check out https://studentaid.gov/h/apply-for-aid/fafsa to see how to get started.
- Compare offers from different schools—one school may be able to match or improve on another school's financial aid offer.
- Keep your grades up—a good grade point average (GPA) helps a lot when it comes to merit scholarships and grants.
- You have to reapply for financial aid every year, so you'll be filling out that FAFSA form again!
- Look for ways that loans might be deferred or forgiven—service commitment programs are a way to use service to repay loans.

While You're in College

Of course, while you're enrolled in a college program, you'll take all the courses required to graduate. But don't stop there. You'll have elective credits, too. Think about other subjects that could come in handy for you as a trades professional—first as an apprentice and journey-level electrician and, most of all, when you reach the rank of master electrician. The following courses can help you run your own electrician business effectively and work well with customers, coworkers, employers, and employees:

- Small business
- Marketing
- Communications

One of the best ways to keep college costs down is to study hard and do well in your classes. Sometimes, young people get to college and think it's the time to break loose, party, and just have fun. There's plenty of time for fun, but what happens if you have too much fun and fail a class? To graduate, you'll have to take that class again—that means paying for it twice! Putting in the work to get good grades translates quickly into lower school costs and a better chance at a high-paying job later on.

Summary

Like all the skilled trades, working as an electrician combines hands-on training with lifelong learning. As an apprentice electrician, you'll need to put in some hours in the classroom to learn all the ins and outs of electrical technology and the National Electrical Code *in the right order* and *with all topics covered.* After you have your license, you'll need to build on that learning with additional courses to maintain your journey-level or master's license. It's important to stay up to date on the latest developments, materials, practices, code changes, and especially safety.

Electricians are in high demand. There is plenty of financial aid available to you through employers, state funds, and scholarships. Training and associate's degree programs for electricians are primarily offered through community and technical colleges, which already have much lower tuition than four-year colleges and universities. Credit transfer makes moving into a bachelor's degree program afterward much more affordable.

With so much in your favor, you should easily finish your electrician training without much student debt—quite possibly with no debt at all. The financial side of being an electrician is all in your favor.

In chapter 4, we will look at what goes into getting a job as an electrician and the skills you'll need to succeed as an electrician at all levels.

JESS MORTON, THEATER ELECTRICIAN

Jessica Morton.
Courtesy of Jessica Morton

Jessica Morton is a theater electrician. She holds a BA in theater from Marymount Manhattan College. As a member of the International Alliance of Theatrical Stage Employees (IATSE) Local 1, the stagehands union for New York City, Jess is able to work as a freelance independent contractor while still receiving the protections and benefits that come with union membership. She is certified by the Entertainment Technician Certification Program (ETCP). Jess has a long list of credits on theatrical productions, including such jobs as electrician, programmer, spotlight operator, deck electrician/moving light tech, light board operator, and assistant electrician. When not at work on a theater project, she and her husband are renovating a house in northern New Jersey.

What does a theater electrician do?

There's a ton of stuff this job encompasses. The main difference between a theater electrician and what most people think of as an electrician is that most of what we do is temporary wiring. So you're not licensed the same way you are for working within the walls of a home. We're doing very large-scale extension cords and lights. Physically, nothing is buried inside of walls, so it counts as "temporary" even if it's a permanent installation in a space. If wiring is getting put behind the walls, you have a licensed electrician come out and do that or inspect it. It's an arts job, even though it's the technical part of an arts job.

How did you decide to become a theater electrician?

I didn't know it was a career at first! I was at Marymount Manhattan College in New York City. Marymount is a small school, so they encouraged you to go out and be a part of theater in the city. They had a board of internships that arranged for me to intern on a one-man show in a theater off Broadway. I showed up for my internship with no idea what the job was. They said, "How do you feel about ladders?" and I said, "Good." They asked if I had a crescent wrench, so I brought a small one from home. The lighting designer showed me what I would be doing, and I loved it from the very first day. It was an unpaid internship except for the subway tokens so I could get back and forth. The lighting designer liked me and asked me to come back for another show. Then I started getting hired off-Broadway. It's very much a word-of-mouth business. You're on a crew with someone and then they do another job and suggest you for it. I started working full time while I was still in college. It became a career very quickly for me.

What is a typical day on your job?

There are a lot of different things happening, depending on where a show is in the process. I used to work in the rental shops, where you rent equipment for the show. I was working for the show, not for the shops. There's a lot of breaking things up into their appropriate boxes. In a large venue, you might be bringing things in through different doors on different streets. Depending on the size of the show, it could be six weeks in the shop or just a couple of days.

Once you get into the theater, you're doing a "load-in"—essentially taking the light plot (the lighting plan) and making sure you're getting all the lights to where they need to go and that the light board can control the individual lights or group lights. You're reading and following the plans. In the shop, you're standing and moving around in one space. With the load-in, you're all over the theater, in the grid above the theater sixty feet up, on ladders, maybe in harness somewhere hauling lights and cable around, dropping cable through the ceiling. That's the very physical part of our job. Those are the times your Fitbit is registering ridiculous numbers!

The next step is "focus," when the designers get into the building. You start turning lights on, making sure they're pointed where they need to point, that the color is correct, that they're shuttered into the right place on the stage. There's usually a handful of people doing the actual focus and a larger group supporting them, holding ladders, running around for bits and pieces, moving lights and things if the theater architecture doesn't quite match what they're expecting. That's where the artistic part of it comes in.

Then you have a period called "tech," where the lighting designer is writing cues for the show, and programmers are setting cues in the computer for the stationary and moving lights, and spotlights operators are getting their cues, seeing what works and what doesn't. When I've been the light board operator, I've sometimes also been the programmer, which is often a separate job. Sometimes I've been the deck electrician, working with electrified props on stage or a fog machine, things like that. That's a lot of fun because you're backstage with all the craziness of the cast and the stage manager and wardrobe. That's the social part that I like.

Once the show has closed, there's the "load-out," which is much quicker than load-in. It's just putting everything back in the box and sending it back to the rental shop.

There are other jobs that fall into the electrician category that I don't do, like video and sound. Those are outside the scope of what I do.

There are days where I'm in the shop during the day for one show and then working on another show at night. Some people work eighty-hour weeks. I used to do that, but then I decided I wanted to do more other things, stretch other parts of my brain, and not stress my body so much.

The tech process on any show starts at 8:00 a.m. and ends around midnight. That's the long and exhausting part of the process for us. I also work on events, on Fashion Week. I've done almost no TV and no film. All of those things go into the stagehand/theater electrician category as well.

What's the best part of being a theater electrician?

I really love being a part of the arts but also having a technical job that makes me work my body and my brain in a linear, technical way. I'm not a creative person by nature, but I love being part of the creative process. I love troubleshooting gear. It gives me the best of both worlds. Running spotlight is one of the most artistic jobs in the theater (like the sound mixer). At that point, you begin to be able to see what someone means and see what the intention is.

What's the most challenging part of being a theater electrician?

The hours! The fact that sometimes it's excessively long hours, and you're just exhausted. For people who have families or friends outside of the business, it's very difficult, because you're often working nights and weekends. So all those weddings and other events that everyone else gets to go to, you miss those. Or if your kid is sick, you can't stay home. Once the show starts, you are *there*.

What's the most surprising thing about being a theater electrician?

The most surprising thing is that it was a job. I didn't know I could do it as a career. Within the job, at the start of this, I didn't know how much I would have to keep up with the technology. As you get into larger scale, there are new kinds of lights and lightboards, new ways of controlling things, and you're constantly trying to keep up with that. The union has a technology fund, so they offer a lot of classes. If you're out doing shopwork, you drop by the different areas in the shop and talk to people about what they're doing. When you see something new come into the building, you talk to the person in charge of it. I try to (when there's time) hover with those people or pair up with them and be their support person, so I can see it and learn about it. A lot of the manufacturers have classes or information online. Sometimes I'll learn about a light when I have to take it apart—I sit with the manual and a YouTube video or call a friend and figure it out. It's a very hands-on learning process for most of that.

How did (or didn't) your education prepare you to be a theater electrician?

My particular school didn't have a technical program. They had a little bit of a design program and a class combining lighting and sound. My school didn't teach me about electrics work; it taught me about theater. It prepared me by letting me out into the world while I was still in school. There are schools that have technical programs, which is a great way of networking. The theater camp I went to growing up—the technical stuff got done behind the scenes without us really knowing. My husband had a very different experience—he joined the stage crew when he was in high school and learned so much. A lot of the people who did that with him in high school went on to study it in college and do this professionally.

I think going to a trade school and learning about electricity is potentially a way to get to this as well. So much hands-on learning. I was talking to a group that's trying to increase equity in theater tech, and they were saying they get calls from people who ask if they can just come and watch. I have gotten calls like that, too: "Can you show this kid around?"

Is being a theater electrician what you expected?

Since I started working on this before I knew it was a career, I never really had a chance to have an expectation of the job. So it's just sort of evolved on its own. It's definitely not what I expected from a job in theater, because I expected I would have to be on the creative end if I wanted a job in theater.

What's next? Where do you see yourself going from here?

I'm very happy with where I've gotten to. I don't particularly see changing what I do within this job. If I can keep up with the technology, I think I can keep up with the job. I'm working on Broadway shows. I'm in a union that has health care, that has a retirement plan. I don't have to fight for my salary with every job, and I can work many different places. I'd like to work this particular path through retirement—maybe with less heavy lifting as I get older.

Where do you see the career of theater electrician going from here?

I see a lot more technology being added to it, so the people getting hired are the ones who can really understand that. It tends to cut down on the number of jobs while the show is actually happening. But you're getting all this crazy and heavy gear, so you have just as many people putting the show together.

What is your advice for a young person considering this career?

I would say there are a lot of different routes to this job. If you are interested in it, any one of them can get you there. Make an effort to meet people; go introduce yourself to people. That doesn't have to be "Will you hire me?" But contact people at the theater and ask if you can watch. There are smaller theaters that have internships, summer stock; your local theater—just call them and say you want to help do the lights or put the scenery together. Then be ready for long hours and physically hard work combined with time when you're just waiting for a long time so you can jump in when the actors are offstage. And be OK with both things. Start looking into the technology. The wonderful world of YouTube! There are so many videos and so much media out there to show you what people do with their different gear. You can start to get an idea of what you want to focus on. If you show up with a knowledge of that gear, it puts you ahead of a lot of people.

4

Writing Your Résumé and Interviewing

Stepping into the Working World

Through your courses and apprenticeship, you'll learn all the technical know-how you need to be a successful electrician. And you've already heard about how being an electrician is a great career with lots and lots of opportunity.

From the very first chapter, you've been thinking about what kind of electrician you want to be. Residential? Commercial? Electrical contractor? Specialist? And you've read about what you need to do to reach each level, from apprentice to journey level to master electrician. You've also been thinking about what kind of work environment would suit you best, where in the country you want to live, and what you need to do to get licensed there.

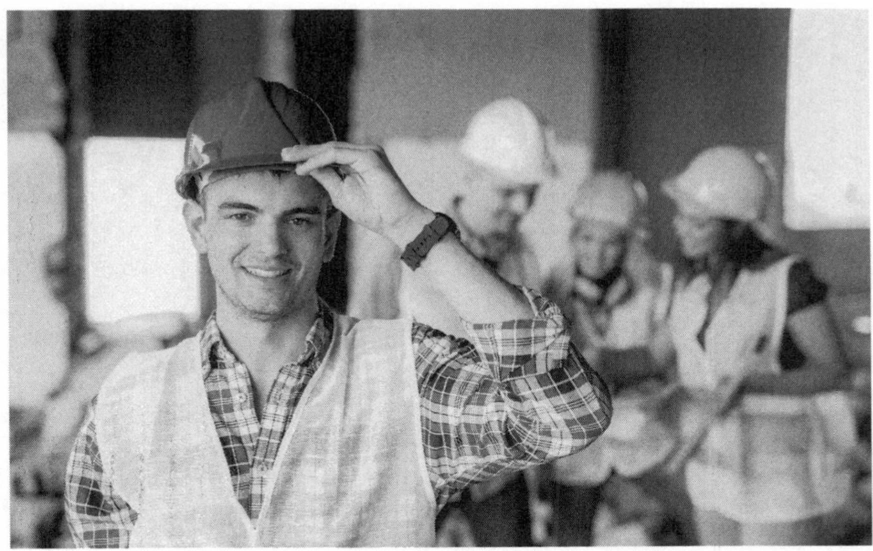

Making a good first impression is important! *MilanMarkovic/iStock/Getty Images*

In this chapter, we're going to take a look at the other skills you need to get not just *a* job, but *the* job. Those are the business skills that everyone—including electricians—needs to have to be successful.

Many electricians, especially residential electricians, work for themselves as sole proprietors of their own businesses. This may grow into being the owner of an electrician business, with apprentices and employees of your own. If you think that might be the path for you, don't miss the section "Things Every Self-Employed Person Needs to Know" later in this chapter.

Where to Find Electrician Jobs

Where do you begin your job search? How do you find companies that are hiring? Don't worry—jobs for electricians are everywhere!

Just as you did in chapter 2, it helps to make yourself a list of what you're looking for in a job and the potential resources that can help you find the right job.

Start with Who You Know

You already know plenty of people in the industry.

- The electrician who invested so much time and resources into training you during your apprenticeship may want to hire you as a journey-level electrician after you pass your exam and get your license.
- If the master electrician who supervised your apprenticeship isn't hiring right now, ask if he or she knows someone else who is hiring and if he or she will give you an introduction and a reference.
- The school where you took your courses probably has an employment or career office where job listings are available to students.
- Let your friends and family know that you're available. There may be an opening where they work, or they may know someone you can talk to.

Check the Listings

There are always lots of jobs for electricians listed in various places on the internet. You just need to use the right search terms, such as the level you're looking for and the location you want to work in. (If you qualified in one state but hope to move to another, be sure the two states have a reciprocity agreement.)

Here are just a few of the options.

LINKEDIN

Create a LinkedIn page for yourself and fill it up with all your qualifications and experience. Then click on "Jobs" on the menu at the top of the page and fill in the keywords and location in the boxes that appear. LinkedIn is a useful site because you can do more than just upload your résumé—you can also maintain professional connections with other people and businesses.

RÉSUMÉ SITES

There are many sites on the internet where you can upload your résumé (you'll learn more about this later in this chapter). It doesn't cost you anything to upload your résumé to these sites. Don't use one that charges you. Some of the most recognized include the following (in alphabetical order):

- CareerBuilder
- Glassdoor
- Indeed
- Monster
- TheMuse
- ZipRecruiter

DIRECT SEARCH

If you don't want to post your résumé on the internet, enter search terms into your favorite search engine and job listings from those sites will come up. Try things like:

- journeyman electrician jobs near me
- licensed electrician jobs near me
- licensed electrician jobs [city where you want to live]
- electrical contractors hiring near me

COMPANY WEBSITES

Most larger employers (and even some small ones) have a page on their website labeled "Careers" or "Work with Us" or "Employment," which contains information about current job openings and how to apply for them.

UNIONS AND PROFESSIONAL ORGANIZATIONS

One of the benefits of belonging to a union or a professional association is access to current job listings. If you already belong to a union like the International Brotherhood of Electrical Workers (IBEW), for instance, you can use its search tool to find other union jobs.

Writing Your Résumé

Does an electrician need a résumé? Yes, indeed! Everybody needs a résumé. Even if the job you're applying for wants you to fill in an online application form, your résumé contains all the information they want in one place.

What Is a Résumé?

A résumé is a brief written list of what you've done and where you learned to do it. It may also include any honors you've earned or special things you've done or been a part of. A printed résumé usually should be one to two pages long.

You submit your résumé (along with a cover letter) whenever you apply for a job. You may also want to upload your résumé to a few of the many résumé sites available on the internet and use it as the basis for a page on LinkedIn.

For an electrician's résumé, you want to be sure to include where you learned the trade, who you did your apprenticeship with, what special skills you have (with the ones you do best at the top), any specialized certifications you hold, and union membership (if you're a union member), as well as your employment history.

Types of Résumés

There are three basic formats for a résumé.

REVERSE CHRONOLOGICAL RÉSUMÉ

The reverse chronological résumé is the most traditional format. It's written with the most current information first, going backward to the oldest information last. This type of résumé works for everyone, whether you're a student, an apprentice, a journeyworker, or a master at your trade. It's the easiest to use when you want to fill in an online or paper application form. The usual layout is fairly simple.

- Name and contact information at the top
- Education, starting with most recent first (apprenticeship, college, high school). When you're at the beginning of your career, list education first. When you're more experienced, move the education section after the experience section
- Qualifications such as certification and/or license
- Professional experience with job title, dates of employment (month or year is fine), and a short bulleted list of your duties and accomplishments. Be sure to include the things you accomplished or achieved in those roles
- Military service (if any)
- Awards and honors (if any)
- Volunteer experience (if relevant)

FUNCTIONAL RÉSUMÉ

A functional résumé is designed to highlight your skills and qualifications rather than your work history. Also called a skills résumé, the functional résumé shows that you're a strong candidate for a job, plays down periods of time when you weren't employed, and helps employers focus on specific skills needed for the job they're hiring for.

You might use a functional résumé if you spent part of your working years in a different kind of job. For instance, if you were an actor before becoming a theater electrician or if you had made jewelry before becoming a residential electrician, you might want to use a functional résumé to highlight your electrician skills or to tie in interesting or important skills (like customer service!) that you picked up in other jobs. It's all about making sure the employer can focus on what's relevant to the job in question.

For a functional résumé, break up your résumé information into several categories that describe your skills. The categories should be in order of importance to the *potential employer*. Within each category, you'll include a bulleted list of examples. These should be in order of importance, as well, rather than in chronological order. Include a synopsis of your work experience. The usual layout for a functional résumé follows.

- Name and contact information at the top
- Summary of your skills and abilities
- Qualifications such as certification and licensing
- Awards and honors (if any)
- Relevant skill blocks in order of importance, such as technical skills, business skills, people skills
- Professional experience with job titles, dates of employment (month or year is fine). Include short bulleted items listing your duties and accomplishments if the jobs are different from each other in a significant way (otherwise you've already covered this in the skill blocks).
- Education, starting with most recent first (if you've been to college, you don't need to list your high school).
- Volunteer experience (if relevant)

COMBINED RÉSUMÉ

A combined résumé is the best of both worlds. It combines aspects of both the reverse chronological résumé and the functional résumé. A combined résumé is best for someone who has developed enough experience that it can be summarized. It highlights your skills while still showing your impressive employment history.

Like a functional résumé, the combined résumé begins with a professional summary of your skills, abilities, and achievements, which are specifically relevant to the job opening. Then your education and experience follow in reverse chronological order.

Use a combined résumé when

- You want to focus on your knowledge and accomplishments
- You want to highlight your relevant experience
- You're applying for a job that requires technical skills and expertise (like being an electrician)
- You want to move into a new field (like being an electrician)
- You want to demonstrate mastery in your field

The usual layout for a combined résumé is simple.

- Name and contact information at the top
- Summary of your skills and abilities
- Qualifications such as certification and licensing
- Professional experience with job titles and dates of employment (month or year is fine). Include short bulleted items about your duties and accomplishments if the jobs are significantly different from each other (otherwise you've already covered this in the skill blocks)
- Awards and honors (if any)
- Education, starting with your apprenticeship, then trade school, then high school
- Volunteer experience (if relevant)

Writing Your Cover Letter

Your cover letter is a short, personalized letter sent along with your résumé to introduce yourself to a potential employer. A well-written cover letter is a way to show a little of your personality, to highlight where and how your background makes you a good fit for the position, and to indicate your interest in working for that employer.

You should always try to send your cover letter (with your résumé) to the person who is responsible for making hiring decisions. Only if you absolutely cannot find out who that person is should you send it to the human resources office.

Your letter should be in business letter format (see the sample business letter on page 89).

- Be sure your name and contact information are at the top of the letter, either centered or on the right.
- Address the reader by name—avoid generic greetings like "Dear Manager" or "Dear Director." Use Ms. or Mr. with the last name. (Do not use Miss or Mrs. unless you have been specifically instructed to do so.)
- Identify the specific position you are interested in and where you heard about it (some companies like to track how applicants hear about positions so they know which recruiting methods are working best). Mention that your résumé is included or attached.
- If you heard about the opening from a specific person, mention that person by name.
- Highlight your most relevant qualifications: skills that match the ones in the job description and skills that could transfer to those in the job description. Focus on your strengths and on what you could bring to the position. Think about this from the employer's position—what about your background will benefit them?
- Avoid negative language—phrase everything in a positive way. In particular, avoid complaining about a previous employer or customer.
- Your conclusion should include a confident call to action, such as a request for an interview. Don't ask directly for the job, just an interview at this point. Include your phone number here, as well as with your contact information at the top.
- Closing: Sincerely, (That's it. Don't use any other word.)
- Add a few lines of space for your signature, then type your name.
- Sign the letter by hand.

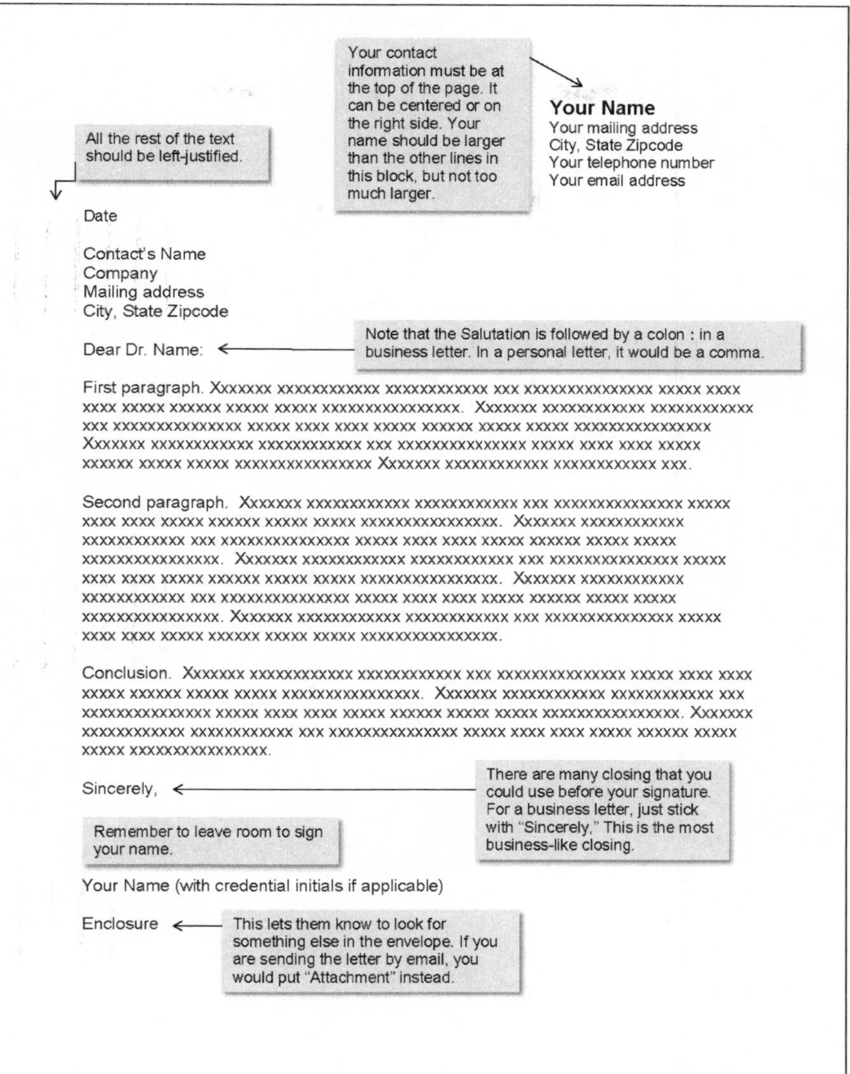

Your contact information must be at the top of the page. It can be centered or on the right side. Your name should be larger than the other lines in this block, but not too much larger.

Your Name
Your mailing address
City, State Zipcode
Your telephone number
Your email address

All the rest of the text should be left-justified.

Date

Contact's Name
Company
Mailing address
City, State Zipcode

Dear Dr. Name:

Note that the Salutation is followed by a colon : in a business letter. In a personal letter, it would be a comma.

First paragraph. Xxxxxxx xxxxxxxxxxxx xxxxxxxxxxxx xxx xxxxxxxxxxxxxxx xxxxx xxxx xxxx xxxxx xxxxxx xxxxx xxxxx xxxxxxxxxxxxxxxx. Xxxxxxx xxxxxxxxxxxx xxxxxxxxxxxx xxx xxxxxxxxxxxxxxx xxxxx xxxx xxxx xxxxx xxxxxx xxxxx xxxxx xxxxxxxxxxxxxxxx Xxxxxxx xxxxxxxxxxxx xxxxxxxxxxxx xxx xxxxxxxxxxxxxxx xxxxx xxxx xxxx xxxxx xxxxxx xxxxx xxxxx xxxxxxxxxxxxxxxx Xxxxxxx xxxxxxxxxxxx xxxxxxxxxxxx xxx.

Second paragraph. Xxxxxxx xxxxxxxxxxxx xxxxxxxxxxxx xxx xxxxxxxxxxxxxxx xxxxx xxxx xxxx xxxxx xxxxxx xxxxx xxxxx xxxxxxxxxxxxxxxx. Xxxxxxx xxxxxxxxxxxx xxxxxxxxxxxx xxx xxxxxxxxxxxxxxx xxxxx xxxx xxxx xxxxx xxxxxx xxxxx xxxxx xxxxxxxxxxxxxxxx. Xxxxxxx xxxxxxxxxxxx xxxxxxxxxxxx xxx xxxxxxxxxxxxxxx xxxxx xxxx xxxx xxxxx xxxxxx xxxxx xxxxx xxxxxxxxxxxxxxxx. Xxxxxxx xxxxxxxxxxxx xxxxxxxxxxxx xxx xxxxxxxxxxxxxxx xxxxx xxxx xxxx xxxxx xxxxxx xxxxx xxxxx xxxxxxxxxxxxxxxx. Xxxxxxx xxxxxxxxxxxx xxxxxxxxxxxx xxx xxxxxxxxxxxxxxx xxxxx xxxx xxxx xxxxx xxxxxx xxxxx xxxxx xxxxxxxxxxxxxxxx.

Conclusion. Xxxxxxx xxxxxxxxxxxx xxxxxxxxxxxx xxx xxxxxxxxxxxxxxx xxxxx xxxx xxxx xxxxx xxxxxx xxxxx xxxxx xxxxxxxxxxxxxxxx. Xxxxxxx xxxxxxxxxxxx xxxxxxxxxxxx xxx xxxxxxxxxxxxxxx xxxxx xxxx xxxx xxxxx xxxxxx xxxxx xxxxx xxxxxxxxxxxxxxxx. Xxxxxxx xxxxxxxxxxxx xxxxxxxxxxxx xxx xxxxxxxxxxxxxxx xxxxx xxxx xxxx xxxxx xxxxxx xxxxx xxxxx xxxxxxxxxxxxxxxx.

Sincerely,

There are many closing that you could use before your signature. For a business letter, just stick with "Sincerely," This is the most business-like closing.

Remember to leave room to sign your name.

Your Name (with credential initials if applicable)

Enclosure

This lets them know to look for something else in the envelope. If you are sending the letter by email, you would put "Attachment" instead.

A business letter always follows the same format. *Courtesy of the author*

Application Forms

There's a good chance you'll be filling in an online application form. Larger companies or commercial employers may have their own online forms. Others may use the forms provided by online résumé or hiring services. Small companies may want you to fill in a paper application form.

As long as you keep your résumé up to date, you shouldn't have any trouble filling in these forms, because the information asked for on the form is the same information you already have on your résumé.

Online Application Forms

Online application forms make things easier for applicants and employers. One advantage is that you can often copy and paste information from your résumé, which should be saved on your computer, directly into the right box on the form; however, online forms can be unforgiving about what information they want and how they want you to provide it.

- Be sure to fill in all the boxes that are required—often marked with an asterisk (*).
- Fill in nonrequired boxes as best you can.
- If there is a place to upload your résumé, do that as well as filling in the form.
- Online forms are not perfect. For instance, if they ask for a letter, résumé, and list of references but only give you a place to upload the résumé, try saving all the documents together (in that order) in a PDF file and upload them as one file.
- Be sure you have filled in everything correctly before you hit "send."
- If you have any trouble with the form, call the company (usually the human resources or personnel office) and ask for help.

Paper Application Forms

Paper forms are a lot less common than they once were, but you still encounter them, especially at smaller employers. You'll need to copy information by hand from your résumé onto the paper form.

- Write neatly. Paper forms are read by people. Keep information in the appropriate boxes.
- Fill in all required information.
- Fill in as much nonrequired information as you have.
- Attach your cover letter and your résumé if possible.
- Paper application forms are usually completed on site, at the potential employer's office, so if you have a problem or a question about the form, there may be someone you can ask. Be sure to ask.
- Be sure everything on the form is correct before you submit it.
- If you make a mess of the form, with lots of changes and crossing out, ask for a new form and fill it in neatly.

GETTING TO YES

There is a lot of work for electricians, and you will most certainly find a job. But there's no guarantee that you will be offered the job of your dreams when you first start looking. Here are some tips that will improve your chances of "getting to yes."

- Do your research—find out about the company that you want to apply to.
- Talk to people—especially people you know already or friends of friends.
- Ask about what the potential employer is like to work for.
- Ask about what the employer values in employees.
- Ask about benefits and the general pros and cons of working there.
- If there is a specific job opening you're qualified for, apply for it!
- If there isn't a specific job opening, send a letter to the head of the company or department you're interested in, mention your contacts, and ask if they would speak with you about potential openings.
- Be flexible—you might find a good job in a different location than you wanted or by doing something slightly different than you originally planned.
- Put your best self forward—everyone you meet is a potential contact for a job (or maybe just a new friend).
- If you get an interview, don't forget that all-important thank-you note! It's one of the most important things you can do to make a good impression. Send the note *that day*, as soon as possible after the interview occurs.
- Don't put all of your eggs in one basket—apply for numerous jobs at the same time.

DEALING WITH NO

A wise person once said, "If they didn't hire you, you probably would not have been happy working there anyway." Both employers and employees need to find the right fit. If they didn't think you were the right fit, you most likely wouldn't have thought so after a while, either. Here are some tips to weather the noes while you're waiting for the yeses.

- Apply for lots of jobs at the same time, so no particular job is too important to you.
- It doesn't feel great to be turned down for a job but try not to take it personally.
- Don't burn your bridges! Don't retaliate with an angry letter or email or troll the company all over social media. Another opportunity may come up there or through that company.
- Keep improving your résumé and your cover letter.
- Keep putting your best self forward—even if you're feeling discouraged, pick up your head and move through your day shining with confidence.
- Work your contacts—talk to other people you know. They may know an employer who would be a great fit for you.
- Take advice—if someone (especially at or following an interview) tells you that you need to improve something, *improve it*. This may be an additional skill you need to learn; it may be something about your interpersonal skills, your spelling, your breath, or whatever. If someone tells you something about yourself that you don't like to hear but suspect may be right, don't get mad. Get better.
- Keep doing your research so if one employer turns you down, you have three more to apply to that day.
- Keep telling yourself that employment is just around the corner. Then make it true!

The Interview

An interview is a business meeting where a prospective employer is checking you out. Don't forget that you are also checking the employer out. You both are there to see if it would be a good fit for you to work together. No matter how much you want the job, remember that you are not there to beg for charity—you are there to offer your services in your professional role.

As an electrician, you are in high demand. But it's still important to make a good impression when you're applying for a job at any level. Be your best self, be confident, be polite.

Interviewing Tips

- **Be on time**—don't be late, *ever*. Try to arrive ten to fifteen minutes early so that you have time to go to the restroom and check yourself in the mirror before you go into the interview. But don't be *too* early—that's just awkward.
- **Dress appropriately**—see "What to Wear" later in this chapter for tips about how to dress.
- **Take your résumé**—yes, they already have it. But bring extra copies just in case. It's helpful and shows that you're the kind of person who is prepared.
- **Smile**—let them know that you will be a pleasant person to work with.
- **Shake hands well**—a firm handshake marks you as a person to be taken seriously. It's traditional to shake hands as you enter the meeting and again before you leave. See "To Shake or Not to Shake?" on page 94.
- **Ask for a business card**—you may meet with just one person, a committee, or several people individually. At the end of the meeting, ask for a business card from each person so that you have good contact information for your thank-you notes (see "Following Up" later in this chapter).
- **Have good posture**—sit up straight, make reasonable eye contact (not staring, not avoiding), keep your shoulders back. Make it look normal, though—like you always sit or stand that way. Good posture conveys

TO SHAKE OR NOT TO SHAKE?

A handshake is a traditional form of greeting, especially in business. When you arrive for a job interview—or just meet someone new—a good, firm handshake shows that you are a person to be taken seriously.

But shaking hands is not done in every culture, and even in North America, the norm of shaking hands has changed. During the COVID-19 crisis in 2020, people stopped shaking hands to avoid spreading germs. As things get back to normal, some people will want to resume shaking hands and some people won't.

When you arrive for a job interview, follow the lead of the person you're meeting with. A respectful head nod is just fine.

The same is true when you're meeting with customers. If they offer to shake hands, do so if you're comfortable. If they don't want to shake hands, then don't. And don't be offended—it's nothing personal!

Shaking hands in the twenty-first century is something to think about. *Cineberg/iStock/Getty Images*

energy and enthusiasm for the job, as well as showing that you have the physical strength to do what electricians do.

- **Be prepared**—learn about the company ahead of time so that you sound knowledgeable during the interview. Read their website; talk to people.
- **Be ready to answer questions**—at an electrician job interview, you can expect to be asked some standard questions ("Where do you see yourself in five years?") and questions about the work that show that you know your stuff.
- **Don't be afraid to ask questions**—some people don't like to ask questions in an interview because they think it makes them look ignorant. However, not asking questions actually can make them appear to be uninterested. Have some questions prepared—both basic and in depth, because the basic ones might get answered before you have a chance to ask them.
- **Stay off your phone**—does it really have to be said? If you're looking at your phone during an interview, you'll look like you don't care. Nobody wants to hire someone who doesn't care!

What to Wear

As an electrician, you'll wear hard-wearing work clothes to the jobsite, like work pants, steel-toed boots, work shirts, coveralls, and safety equipment such as a hard hat. So what should you wear to a job interview? The answer is "business casual," which can mean different things for different places. You don't need to be fancy, but you should be presentable.

- If you're applying for a job as an apprentice or journey-level electrician with a smaller company, you could wear jeans and a nice button-down shirt or blouse. You can wear work boots instead of shoes, as long as they're clean.
- If you're applying for a job at a larger company, especially with an electrical contractor or at a business, organization, or institution that is not primarily an electrician company, you should wear khakis instead of jeans and a nice shirt or sweater. Men should add a tie, and women might wear some simple jewelry. Nice but simple shoes.

- *Always* be clean and neat for an interview. Brush your teeth. Shower, wash your hair, get a fresh haircut, or pull long hair back neatly. Avoid cologne and cigarette smoke. Don't chew gum.

Tip: T-shirts may be appropriate for your workplace, especially worn under coveralls or a uniform. But message tees are never appropriate for work. Leave the ones with words, pictures, jokes, political or religious messages, cartoons, and so forth at home. What's funny to you could be offensive to a customer, coworker, or your boss. Being offensive is unprofessional.

What Employers Look For

There are certain qualities that every skilled tradesperson should have. During a job interview, potential employers are assessing you for these characteristics. Ask yourself these questions and if you think you need to get better at something, then get better!

COMMUNICATION AND SOCIAL SKILLS

- Will you be able to understand the customer's problems, needs, and values?
- Will you be able to work well with your boss and coworkers?
- Do you have active listening skills?
- Do you speak clearly?
- Do you write clearly?
- Do you show politeness, friendliness, and a good attitude?

GOOD WORK ETHIC

- Do you work hard at assigned tasks?
- Do you look for ways to help employers, coworkers, or customers beyond assigned tasks?
- Do you look for ways to improve your performance?
- Are you on time?

- Do you work well and thoroughly until the job is done or watch the clock to see how soon you can leave?
- Do you show initiative and work to solve problems?

ADAPTABILITY

- Are you flexible about new situations, new rules and regulations, and new or different environments?
- Are you willing and eager to learn the latest developments, processes, procedures, and code updates?
- Can you get along with all kinds of people?

ENTHUSIASM FOR YOUR FIELD

- Do you feel good about the work you do as an electrician?
- Do you like solving problems?
- Do you like helping people?
- Do you have a desire to continue to build your skills and learn new things?

> For somebody who's applying for a job, as a business owner I look for three qualities in a new hire. I look for somebody who's humble enough to ask for help when it's needed and let us know when something is seriously wrong. I want somebody who's hungry—they want to work, which isn't that common anymore. I want somebody who's going to keep asking for work and asking for advice on how to do this thing better and faster and easier. The third thing is somebody who's "people smart." A lot of what we do is reading between the lines of what customers say to figure out what they actually need.—Jessica Gray, apprentice electrician

Following Up

After any kind of job interview, it is *extremely important* to follow up. This is what shows the potential employer that you are genuinely interested in the job and in working with there. Write your thank-you note immediately after the interview. Not tomorrow, not later in the week, not sometime soon—*the same day*. Be sure to mention your interest in the job and one or two things from the interview that interested you most. If you met separately with several people, send *each* one of them a *separate* note!

Handwritten Letter

Traditionally, a handwritten letter always has been the gold standard for thank-you notes. (If your handwriting is truly terrible, then type the letter and sign it by hand.) These must be *mailed the same day as your interview*, so be sure you have stamps and envelopes before even going to the interview.

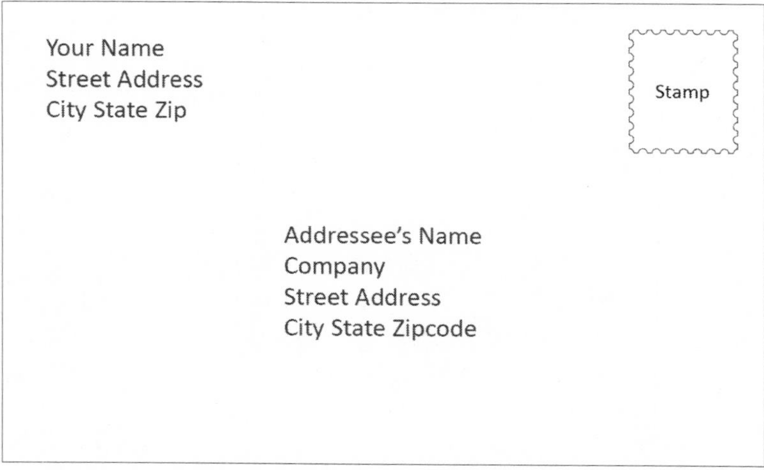

This format is used for all envelopes that will be mailed. *Courtesy of the author*

Emailed Thank-You Notes

Whereas an email is less personal than a hand-signed letter on paper, it's a lot faster and today is considered an acceptable way to communicate. An email should contain the same content as a handwritten letter including—and especially—your enthusiasm about the job.

Tip: Many employers require employees to pass a drug test and a background check. Think about it—nobody wants to find out too late that the tradesperson hired turned out to be a criminal or was impaired while working. Employers need to be sure that their employees are reputable people—there are a lot of safety and liability issues involved with working with electricity. So be sure that you can meet those requirements!

Just like a handwritten note, start with "Dear [Mr. or Ms. Name]"—(replacing "[Mr. or Mrs. Name]" with the appropriate name—and signing it "Sincerely," two hard returns, "[Your Name]." Since you won't write your signature, two line breaks are enough.

On the Job

Now that you've got the job, it's important to keep it! It's not that hard. Just remember these simple tips.

- **Do your best**—an electrician's biggest asset is high-quality work.
- **Be reliable**—ask anyone—a reliable electrician is worth his or her weight in gold and then some.
- **Be on time**—show up on time for work or even a few minutes early.
- **Be prepared**—walk in the door ready to work.
- **Keep good records**—this saves everyone time and money, from your boss to your customers to yourself.
- **Be polite**—treat everyone you meet with the same respect you want to receive.
- **Stay calm**—you do your best work when you're calm, especially if there's a problem to solve. Customers with emergencies may not be able to stay calm, but if you are calm and reassuring, they'll trust you to solve their problem.
- **Have integrity**—be honest and respect other people's persons and property.

Things Every Self-Employed Person Needs to Know

If you think you might want to go into business for yourself as an electrician, there are some very important things that you'll need to take care of for yourself. When you work for an employer, they usually are responsible for making sure that you have health, life, and disability insurance, vacation and sick leave, and a retirement plan. Self-employed people and business owners must stay on top of all those things for themselves (and for their employees, if they have any).

Establishing Your Business

If you go into business for yourself, you'll need a good business plan to get yourself set up. This book can't cover everything you need to know about starting a business, and the rules vary from state to state. But here are some of the things you'll need to know when the time comes.

BUSINESS STRUCTURE

What kind of business entity will you be? According to the U.S. Small Business Administration (SBA), there are seven types of business entities, which can sometimes be combined depending on the rules of your state. Generally, the differences have to do with how many people are involved and who is considered liable (at fault) if anything goes wrong.

Table 4.1. Types of Business Structures

Business Structure	*Ownership*	*Liability*	*Taxes*
Sole proprietorship	One person	Unlimited personal liability	Personal tax only
Partnership	Two or more people	Unlimited personal liability unless structured as a limited partnership	Self-employment tax (except for limited partners); personal tax
Limited liability company (LLC)	One or more people	Owners are not personally liable	Self-employment tax; personal tax or corporate tax

Business Structure	*Ownership*	*Liability*	*Taxes*
Corporation—C corp	One or more people	Owners are not personally liable	Corporate tax
Corporation—S corp	One or more people but no more than 100, and all must be U.S. citizens	Owners are not personally liable	Personal tax
Corporation—B corp	One or more people	Owners are not personally liable	Corporate tax
Corporation—Nonprofit	One or more people	Owners are not personally liable	Tax exempt but corporate profits can't be distributed

KNOW YOUR MARKET

As an entrepreneur you will need to understand your area, the need for electricians where you want to work, who your competition is, and what niche you want to fill in the market.

YOUR BUSINESS NAME

Choose a business name that people will be able to find easily and recognize. Keep it short and easy to spell. Once you choose a name, you need to register it. According to the SBA, once you settle on a name you like, you need to protect it. There are four different ways to register your business name. Each way of registering your name serves a different purpose, and some may be legally required depending on your business structure and location.

- Entity name protects you at the state level
- Trademark protects you at the federal level
- "Doing business as" (DBA) doesn't offer legal protection but might be legally required
- Domain name protects your business website address

Each of these name registrations is legally independent. Most small businesses try to use the same name for each kind of registration, but you're not normally required to.[2]

EMPLOYER ID NUMBER

Even if you work alone and have no employees, you'll still need an employer identification number (EIN), also called your federal tax ID number. You need this number to open a business bank account and to apply for business licenses and permits. As your business grows, you'll need it for almost all the paperwork you need to do for you and your employees.

It doesn't cost anything to register for an EIN. You can apply for this number at the Internal Revenue Service website: https://sa.www4.irs.gov/modiein/individual/index.jsp.

KEEPING UP WITH YOUR PAPERWORK

If you're going into business for yourself, it will be especially important to keep up with your business paperwork. These types of records will help you do that.

INCOME STATEMENT

This is also called a profit-and-loss or P&L statement. This is where you track all your income and expenses for the quarter and for the year. At the bottom (the "bottom line"), you subtract expenses from income. If the number is positive, you've made a net profit. If the number is negative, you've made a net loss.

BALANCE SHEET

A balance sheet is a statement of the assets (what you own), liabilities (what you owe), and capital (the difference between assets and liabilities) at a particular point in time.

CASH FLOW STATEMENT

This is where you track cash in and cash out. This is how you keep track of your ability to meet your financial obligations on a day-to-day basis.

Of course, this is just a short introduction. Be sure to read books on small business and entrepreneurship, take classes, and become an expert on running your business. It's usually worthwhile to hire a bookkeeper or accountant to help you track your finances.

Insurance

As a self-employed small businessperson, there are several types of insurance you will need.

- **Health insurance**—the average monthly cost of an individual or family plan depends on things like which plan you choose, how much your deductible is, how much your copay amounts are, and other factors. It's important to look at all of your options and make a careful decision.
- **Auto insurance**—if you have a car or truck, you have to have insurance. If you use your vehicle for your business, keep track of your mileage, because you can deduct some of those expenses from your income tax.
- **Disability insurance**—if you get hurt or sick and can't work, disability insurance pays a percentage of your regular income. Keep good records, because you have to be able to prove how much money you make in a month or a year. There are both short- and long-term disability insurance policies.
- **Life insurance**—if you have dependents (like a spouse or children), then you need life insurance to help replace your income if you should die. Also, if you want to borrow money for your business, the bank may require you to have life insurance.
- **Liability insurance**—depending on your situation, there are several kinds of liability insurance that might be relevant for your business.
- **Business insurance**—small businesses with employees usually need a comprehensive policy combining property and liability coverage to protect the business structure itself and any business-related equipment against theft or damage and injuries that occur on your premises.

Saving for the Future

When you're young and first starting out in life, it often seems more important to focus on paying your immediate expenses than saving for the future. Retirement seems so far in the future. That's for your grandparents to think about! Why should it matter to you?

Well, the future arrives a lot faster than you expect it! And the sooner you start saving for retirement, the more money you'll have when you retire. Let's take a quick look at the difference between starting to save now and waiting a while. (Note: this book is not a substitute for expert financial or legal advice.)

There are several kinds of retirement plans that individuals can participate in. Here's a short list to give you an idea of what to look into. Bear in mind that these things change all the time, so there may be more or fewer options with different rules and regulations when you're ready to start. The following list is adapted from NerdWallet.com.[3]

- **Traditional or Roth IRA**—best for those who are just starting out or saving less than $6,000 a year. If you're leaving a job to start a business, you can also roll your old 401(k) into an IRA. Contributions to a traditional IRA are tax deductible; there are no deductions for a Roth IRA but withdrawals during retirement are tax free.
- **Solo 401(k)**—best for business owners or self-employed individuals with no employees (except a spouse, if applicable).
- **SEP IRA**—best for self-employed people or small business owners with no or few employees.
- **SIMPLE IRA**—best for larger businesses with up to 100 employees.
- **Defined benefit plan**—best for self-employed individuals with no employees who have a high income and want to save a lot for retirement on an ongoing basis.

Let's take a look at the difference between saving and not saving using some different scenarios from Calculator.net[4] (see table 4.2).

Table 4.2. Comparison of Traditional, SIMPLE, and SEP IRAs (pretax $) by Age

	Annual Contribution	*Annual Rate of Return*	*Retirement Age 65*	*After Tax at Age 65*	*Equal to Today's $*
Age 20	$1,200 ($100/month)	6%	$256,669	$218,168	$57,692
Age 20	$6,000 (annual limit)	6%	$1,277,838	$1,086,162	$287,223
Age 30	$1,200 ($100/month)	6%	$134,490	$114,317	$40,626
Age 30	$6,000 (annual limit)	6%	$669,377	$568,971	$202,203
Age 40	$1,200 ($100/month)	6%	$66,267	$56,327	$26,902
Age 40	$6,000 (annual limit)	6%	$329,616	$280,174	$133,813

We're using a 6 percent annual rate of return because it's a very conservative (low) estimate compared to the types of returns real IRA accounts have been earning in recent decades. The important things to notice are as follows:

- The difference between contributing $100 a month (for a total of $1,200 per year) and contributing the full allowed amount ($6,000 per year)
- The difference at age sixty-five between starting to save in your twenties and starting in your forties

Another thing an employer often provides is matching funds for a 401(k) retirement fund. For instance, if you contribute 10 percent of your salary to your 401(k), your employer might contribute up to another 10 percent, for a total of 20 percent. But when you're self-employed, you have to fund that match yourself. So aim to contribute about 20 percent of your income or more (up to the total amount allowed) to your retirement fund. If you really can't afford that at first, begin with $100 a month and then raise the contribution as your income increases over the years.

How can you afford to do that? It's simple, once you accept the idea of *paying yourself first*. Google that phrase and you'll find hundreds of reputable investment advisors who recommend this process. If you put that $100 (or $500) into your IRA *first*, before you pay any other bills or buy something you want, *you won't even miss it*. And it will be in your IRA, quietly earning you money until you need it when you retire.

Taxes

Paying your taxes is part of running a business. Some people object to paying taxes, but taxes are legally required. (If you think of it as doing your part to contribute to the shared resources of your community, it stings less.) Tax laws are constantly changing, and it is your responsibility to keep track of what you are supposed to pay to whom, when, how much, and how often. An accountant or tax attorney can help you, if you need it.

In general, you'll need to be responsible for the following.

FEDERAL INCOME TAX

Self-employed people are responsible for making quarterly payments toward their own federal income tax. You must also pay self-employment tax to cover your Social Security and Medicare taxes (when you work for an employer, the employer deducts this from your paycheck automatically). Do not miss this important step! You can find everything you need to know about paying taxes as a sole proprietor or an independent contractor at the IRS's Self-Employed Individuals Tax Center page.[5]

STATE INCOME TAX

Some states charge state income tax and some don't. If you itemize your federal income tax, you may be able to deduct your state income tax from your federal income tax. Be sure you understand the rules in your state.

SALES TAX

Sales tax is determined on a state-by-state basis. You need to know whether you must charge sales tax in your state. Be sure you follow the sales tax rules for your town or city as well as for your state, and be sure to factor in the cost of sales tax in your own accounting.

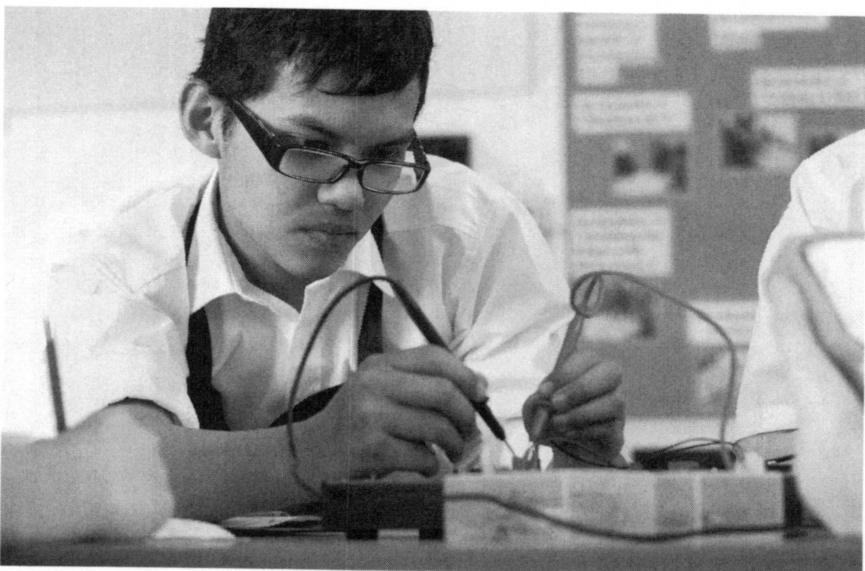

Welcome to the team! *NoSystem images/iStock/Getty Images*

Summary

There is a strong market out there for all the types of electricians we've talked about in this book, and there will continue to be. Whether you work for another electrician, for a business or institution, for an electrical contractor, or go into business for yourself, there will always be work to do and people who need you to do it.

As long as you do a good job and respect the people you work with and work for, you should have a long and lucrative career as an electrician. You'll be figuring out mysteries, solving problems, working with your brain and your hands, and—most important—helping people every day.

Good luck!

JEFF GRAY—MASTER ELECTRICIAN

Jeff Gray. *Courtesy of Grayzer Electric*

Jeff Gray is a master electrician with twenty years of experience. He is the owner of Grayzer Electric in Austin, Texas. His company specializes in residential work, offering everything from residential electrical service and repair to electric car charging stations to estimates on electrical inspections on houses that are up for sale. Jeff believes in educating the public about electricity, so he provides useful tips on Grayzer Electric's website at www.grayzerelectric.com and its Facebook page.

How did you decide to become an electrician?

I always knew that whatever career I chose, I wanted to work with my hands. I briefly considered a career as a mechanic but school for that wasn't opening for some time, so I found work with an electrician, learning on the job. Electrical work just made sense from the get-go, so I continued pursuing it.

What is a typical day on your job?

As a business owner, a typical day for me consists of writing quotes to customers who are looking to have work done, ordering materials for upcoming work, answering any questions the electricians in the field may have, and helping customers understand the way the electricity in their home works.

What's the best part of being an electrician?

The best part for me is being able to work with my hands. I also like the challenge of figuring out how things like electricity work, so it gives me some mental stimulation as well.

What's the most challenging part of being an electrician?

After twenty years in the electrical field, it's tough to find challenging parts for me as an electrician. As a business owner, it can be tough to manage electricians while also juggling things like taxes, purchases, account reconciliation, and customers all at the same time. Working on finding a balance and when to wear which hat is really key.

What's the most surprising thing about being an electrician?

I'm surprised by how little people in general are educated about things that are so common around us. Electricity is something we use every day, arguably something we can't live without, yet the general public doesn't know where it comes from or how it works. As a company we try to spend as much time as we can educating people, so they're more comfortable with the decisions they're making and, hopefully, that education has a ripple effect down to future generations.

How did (or didn't) your education prepare you to be an electrician?

I have a high school diploma and chose to pursue a career instead of higher education. I would say that for me, it's been the best decision I could have made. I would not have been happy sitting in a classroom. I needed to be doing something and becoming an electrician gave me that outlet (pun intended).

Is being an electrician what you expected?

It was a bit like I expected. I expected any trades field to be physically demanding, and it is. But it's also highly rewarding. At the end of the day, I feel like I've accomplished something of significance. I also know that I've made someone's home better and safer than it was before I arrived, which gives me the satisfaction of knowing that I'm making an impact on people in their present and their future.

What's next? Where do you see yourself going from here?

We plan to continue growing Grayzer Electric by hiring and training more residential electricians to not only perform electrical work but to also better educate homeowners.

Where do you see the career of electrician going from here?

Electricity as a whole hasn't really changed all that much over time, and I don't expect it to change drastically anytime soon. As electricians, we've honed the way homes and businesses are wired to a fine science. If I had to take a guess about what could become more important as time passes, I would say alternative energy is a field that's likely to grow in demand.

What is your advice for a young person considering this career?

It's hard work, so be prepared to sweat. Not every day is going to be fun nor will it be easy but it will become easier over time. Electrical work is not something people are born with a talent for; it comes from understanding, so the more you understand, the easier the work will become. You'll suddenly see things in a different light, and that's when it becomes fun.

Notes

Chapter 1

1. Steve Schnute, "How to Become an Electrician: Complete 5 Step Guide," *Ask the Electrical Guy*, https://asktheelectricalguy.com/how-to-become-an-electrician.

2. StateCE blog, "Types of Electricians," May 4, 2018, www.statece.com/blog/profession/types-of-electricians.

3. Bureau of Labor Statistics (BLS), "Occupational Outlook Handbook—Electrical and Electronics Installers and Repairers," last modified September 1, 2020, www.bls.gov/ooh/installation-maintenance-and-repair/electrical-and-electronics-installers-and-repairers.htm#tab-1.

4. Bureau of Labor Statistics (BLS), "Occupational Outlook Handbook—Line Installers and Repairers/Summary," last modified September 1, 2020, www.bls.gov/ooh/installation-maintenance-and-repair/line-installers-and-repairers.htm#tab-3.

5. BLS, "Occupational Outlook Handbook—Line Installers and Repairers/Summary."

6. Bureau of Labor Statistics (BLS), "Occupational Outlook Handbook—Line Installers and Repairers/Pay," last modified September 1, 2020, www.bls.gov/ooh/installation-maintenance-and-repair/line-installers-and-repairers.htm#tab-5.

7. Nikola Tesla, "The Transmission of Electrical Energy without Wires as a Means for Furthering Peace," *Electrical World and Engineer*, January 7, 1905, www.tfcbooks.com/tesla/1905-01-07.htm.

8. U.S. Department of Labor Employment and Training Administration, "U.S. Department of Labor Issues Industry-Recognized Apprenticeship Program Final Rule," press release #20-386-NAT, March 10, 2020, www.dol.gov/newsroom/releases/eta/eta20200310.

9. International Brotherhood of Electrical Workers (IBEW), "Pre-Apprenticeship Programs," 2020, www.ibew.org/Civic-and-Community-Engagement/Pre-Apprenticeships.

10. International Brotherhood of Electrical Workers (IBEW), "Leveling the Playing Field: Pre-Apprenticeships Open Doors to the Middle Class," February 12, 2019, www.ibew.org/media-center/Articles/20Daily/2002/200212_Leveling.

11. Bureau of Labor Statistics (BLS), "Occupational Outlook Handbook—Electricians," www.bls.gov/ooh/construction-and-extraction/electricians.htm#tab-1.

12. Bureau of Labor Statistics (BLS), "Occupational Employment Statistics. Occupational Employment and Wages, May 2019; 47-2111 Electricians," www.bls.gov/oes/current/oes472111.htm#st.

13. Bureau of Labor Statistics (BLS), "Occupational Outlook Handbook—Electricians," www.bls.gov/ooh/construction-and-extraction/electricians.htm#tab-1.

14. Bureau of Labor Statistics (BLS), "Occupational Employment Statistics. Occupational Employment and Wages, May 2019; 47-2111 Electricians," www.bls.gov/oes/current/oes472111.htm#st.

Chapter 2

1. Thomas Edison, quoted in Christine Finn's *Artifacts: An Archaeologist's Year in Silicon Valley* (Cambridge, MA: MIT Press, 2001), 90.

2. Kate Kelly, "Vocational Education in High School: What You Need to Know," Understood: For Learning and Attention Issues website, accessed August 19, 2019, www.understood.org/en/school-learning/choosing-starting-school/finding-right-school/vocational-education-in-high-school.

3. National Center for Construction Education and Research, "NCCER Craft Licensing Map," 2020, www.nccer.org/news-research/reciprocity-map.

4. Colorado Electrical Board, "Electrician Licensure by Examination or Endorsement," https://dpo.colorado.gov/Electrical/Applications.

5. Colorado Electrical Board, "Electrical Board: Continuing Education," https://dpo.colorado.gov/Electrical/CE.

6. Colorado Electrical Board, "Electrical Board."

7. Minnesota Board of Electricity, "Electrical Licensing Basics," www.dli.mn.gov/workers/electrician-or-electrical-installer/electrical-license-experience-and-education.

8. South Dakota Electrical Commission, "Licensing," 2020, https://dlr.sd.gov/electrical/licensing.aspx.

9. Wyoming Department of Fire Prevention and Electrical Safety, "Master Electrician Exam," https://drive.google.com/file/d/1l_LnqZWlyKjNSxGAcA42gyezSZzNmXRN/view.

10. Vermont Department of Public Safety Division of Fire Safety, "Frequently Asked Questions," https://firesafety.vermont.gov/fire-building-safety/boards/electrical/faq.

11. Vermont General Assembly, "The Vermont Statutes Online: 26 V.S.A. § 905. Application; Examinations and Fees," https://legislature.vermont.gov/statutes/section/26/015/00905.

12. Ohio Construction Industry Licensing Board (OCILB), "License Qualification Process," www.com.ohio.gov/dico/OCILB/LicenseQualificationProcess.aspx.

13. Amanda E. Clark, "8 Steps to Better Networking: Making Valuable Connections Is a Skill Every Plumbing Business Owner Should Attempt to Master," *Plumber Magazine*, March 1, 2016, www.plumbermag.com/how-to-articles/sales_residential_marketing_small/8_steps_to_better_networking.

Chapter 3

1. Adapted from information from Manchester Community College, "Electrical Technology," www.mccnh.edu/academics/programs/electrical-technology.

2. GateWay Community College, "Constructions Trades: Electricity," www.gatewaycc.edu/degrees-certificates/applied-technology/construction-trades-electricity-3428-aas.

3. Adapted from information from GateWay Community College, "Constructions Trades: Electricity," www.gatewaycc.edu/degrees-certificates/applied-technology/construction-trades-electricity-3428-aas.

4. Jennifer Ma, Sandy Baum, Matea Pender, and C. J. Libassi, *Trends in College Pricing 2019* (New York: College Board, 2019).

5. GoCollege, "Your Guide to Free Money: College Scholarships," www.gocollege.com/financial-aid/scholarships.

Chapter 4

1. U.S. Small Business Adminstration, "Choose a Business Structure," www.sba.gov/business-guide/launch-your-business/choose-business-structure#section-header-1.

2. U.S. Small Business Adminstration, "Choose Your Business Name," www.sba.gov/business-guide/launch-your-business/choose-your-business-name.

3. Dayana Yochim and Andrea Coombes, "Best Retirement Plans: Choose the Right Account for You," *Nerdwallet*, September 4, 2020, www.nerdwallet.com/blog/investing/best-retirement-plans-for-you.

4. "IRA Calculator," *Calculator.net*, accessed October 8, 2020, www.calculator.net/retirement-calculator.html.

5. "Self-Employed Individuals Tax Center," *Internal Revenue Service*, accessed October 8, 2020, www.irs.gov/businesses/small-businesses-self-employed/self-employed-individuals-tax-center.

Glossary

AAS degree: associate of applied science degree; usually a two-year degree from a community or technical college.

alternating current (AC): electric current that regularly reverses direction many times per second.

ammeter: instrument used to measure the flow of electrical current in amperes; connected in series with the circuit being tested.

ampere (amp): unit of measure for intensity of electric current flowing in a circuit.

apprentice: a person who is learning a trade from a master tradesperson.

apprenticeship: an arrangement (by agreement or contract) in which an apprentice works for and under the tutelage of a master tradesperson to learn a trade or craft.

baccalaureate degree: bachelor's degree.

bachelor's degree: a degree earned by a college or university student after completing a program that usually takes four years.

blue-collar worker: a person who works a job requiring skilled or unskilled manual labor.

certificate: a document issued to show that a person has completed a process or earned or achieved a particular status; in electrical work, a certificate may indicate that a licensed electrician has special expertise in a specific area.

chronological: organized by date from oldest to newest (see reverse chronological).

circuit: closed path around which electrons flow from a voltage or current source; can be in series, parallel, or both.

community college: college that offers general studies and specialized courses to people in a particular community, which can lead to an associate's degree or transfer to a four-year (baccalaureate) college; usually a nonresidential campus.

contact information: name, address, telephone number, email address, or any other means to communicate with another person.

cover letter: a business letter that goes with and explains a resume or other enclosure.

current: flow of an electric charge through a conductor.

diploma: official document awarded by an educational institution that indicates completion of a particular course of study; may or may not be associated with a degree.

electrician: skilled tradesperson who installs, maintains, operates, or repairs electrical equipment.

electron: subatomic particle carrying a negative charge of electricity; rotates around the nucleus of an atom.

EV charger: electric vehicle charging station.

for-profit college: businesses that sell college-level coursework, sometimes leading to a diploma or degree, usually online; the goal is to generate a profit for owners or shareholders, sometimes engaging in predatory student loan practices.

GED: abbreviation for general education diploma, a credential equivalent to a high school diploma that is obtained through testing.

HVAC: abbreviation for "heating, ventilation, and air conditioning" and usually refers to the entire system within a building or structure.

integrated building systems (IBS): systems to integrate all of a building's electrical and power systems to optimize performance and maximize energy efficiency.

journeyworker (journeyperson, journey level, or journeyman): a tradesperson who has completed his or her apprenticeship, finished all required coursework, and passed the licensing examination for his or her trade in the state or municipality to work under the supervision of a master tradesperson.

LEED: abbreviation for Leadership in Energy and Environmental Design, certifies different levels of energy efficiency in building projects, especially new construction.

license, electricians: a permit from the state (or municipality) that shows an electrician has met all the requirements and has all the requisite knowledge to perform electrical work as defined by state or local code.

lineman (line worker): works on power lines, usually at heights up to 180 feet off the ground and at very high voltages up to hundreds of thousands of volts.

master: a tradesperson who has completed all the requirements in his or her state or municipality to hold a license and work independently; a master tradesperson is qualified to train apprentices and hire journey-level tradespeople.

motor: a machine, usually powered by electricity or internal combustion, that provides power for a machine or vehicle.

municipality: a town or city with a local government.

National Electrical Code (NEC): contains the most current standards for the safe installation of electrical wiring and equipment in the United States, including emerging topics such as renewable energy and energy storage. Published by the National Fire Protection Association (NFPA).

networking: forming and maintaining personal connections or relationships with people in your chosen field.

ohm: unit of measure of resistance in a circuit transmitting a current of one ampere when subjected to a potential difference of one volt.

photovoltaic: a method for generating electric power by using solar cells to convert energy from the sun into usable electricity.

private college/university: a nonprofit college or university that does not receive funding from the state in which it is located; also called an "independent" college/university.

public college/university: a nonprofit college (including community, technical, or four-year colleges) or university that receives some of its funding from the state in which it is located.

reciprocity: an agreement between U.S. states by which a professional or tradesperson licensed by one state is also qualified to work in the other state.

repair: fix or mend something that is damaged or faulty.

résumé: an organized list of professional qualifications and accomplishments.

reverse chronological: organized by date from newest to oldest (see chronological).

technical college (technical school): a two-year college that specializes in technical, trades, and general and specialized business courses leading to an associate's degree, licensure, or transfer to a baccalaureate program.

theater electrician: someone who is responsible for the nondesign aspects of theatrical lighting; there are many roles within the theater for theater electricians depending on the scope and needs of the particular production and venue.

trades: jobs that require people who have specific knowledge, skills, and abilities, such as skilled construction trades (including electricians), skilled industrial trades (also including electricians), and skilled service trades.

vocational education: courses or programs that both educate and train students to be able to perform certain types of work, such as a trade or craft; also called technical education.

volt (v): unit measure of voltage; equal to the difference of potential that would drive one ampere of current against one ohm of resistance.

voltage: electromotive force (pressure) causing electrons to flow.

wireman: an electrician licensed (in states with this designation) to work on residential or commercial repairs and installations. Depending on the state, this may be a step between apprentice and journey-level licensing.

Further Resources

This section includes useful resources relating to electrician careers. Of course, this is not a complete list of all the information out there, but these resources will help you to get started finding out more about the craft arts you're interested in.

Being an Electrician

- **ElectricianTrainingHub.com** provides extensive information and advice for people looking to enter the career of electrician.
- **ExploreTheTrades.org** has lots of useful information for anyone considering a career as plumbers, electricians, or HVAC installation and repair experts.
- **Mike Rowe** really wants you to get into the trades! Rowe is known as the host of *Dirty Jobs* on the Discovery Channel and *Somebody's Gotta Do It* on CNN, among many other projects. This chapter could have been devoted entirely to him. Instead, here's a brief sample of what he has to offer:
    - **mikeroweWORKS.org** is Rowe's foundation, which promotes the joy and value of hard work and reconnecting with "the most fundamental elements of civilization—food, energy, education, and the very nature of work itself."
    - **Work Ethic Scholarship Program** is Rowe's scholarship, which is aimed at encouraging hard-working, dedicated, positive students like you to go into the trades. Check it out at www.mikeroweworks.org/scholarship.
- **National Electrical Code (NEC)** by the National Fire Protection Association (NFPA) is the standard source for all the regulations regarding electrical safety. The 2020 edition includes new issues like emergency

disconnects, ground-fault circuit interrupter protection, surge protection, power over ethernet, etcetera.

- **U.S. Bureau of Labor Statistics *Occupational Outlook Handbook*** is an online source that provides information and statistics on all kinds of jobs, including electrician and many related careers. It's easy to understand, with summaries of the job and tabs for more information about things like pay, job outlook, work environment, and more. Start your search at www.bls.gov/ooh.

College and Financial Aid

Learn more about going to college and scholarship options at these websites.

AccreditedSchoolsOnline.org: Funding Your Vocational Degree
www.accreditedschoolsonline.org/vocational-trade-school/financial-aid-scholarships

American Indian College Fund: Provides scholarships and college information for Native American students at any of the nation's thirty-three accredited tribal colleges and universities.
https://collegefund.org

American Indian Graduate Center and AIGCS: Scholarship for Native American students in the United States at the high school, undergraduate, and graduate level.
www.aigcs.org

APIA Scholars: Nonprofit organization that provides college scholarships for Asian Americans and Pacific Islanders (AAPI).
https://apiascholars.org

Cappex: A free website where you can find out about colleges and merit aid scholarships.
www.cappex.com

CashCourse: "Your real-life money guide"—financial information, education, and tools to help you learn about your financial options.
www.cashcourse.org

Chegg: Website with searchable information about scholarships and colleges.
www.chegg.com

College Consensus: Top twenty-five trade school scholarships.
www.collegeconsensus.com/scholarships/trade-school-scholarships

CollegeScholarships.org: vocational school scholarships
www.collegescholarships.org/scholarships/vocational-school.htm

Dell Scholars Program: Scholarship and college-completion program that helps students succeed.
www.dellscholars.org

Fastweb: Search website for research on scholarships, internships, colleges etcetera.
www.fastweb.com

Gates Millennium Scholars: Provides scholarships to reduce barriers to college for African American, American Indian/Alaska Native, Asian Pacific Islander American, and Hispanic American students regardless of major.
https://gmsp.org

GoCollege.com: Your guide to free money—college scholarships.
www.gocollege.com/financial-aid/scholarships/types

HS Finder (Hispanic Scholarship Fund): Helps Hispanic/Latinx students find scholarship information.
https://finder.hsf.net

KnowHow2GO: Information about how to get ready and go to college for middle school and high school students and veterans.
http://knowhow2go.acenet.edu

National Society of High School Scholars (NSHSS): Connects students with scholarships, college fairs, internships, career and leadership opportunities, partner discounts, and more. All students are eligible to apply for high school and college scholarships in the areas of academic excellence, entrepreneurship, leadership, literature, medicine, music, STEM, sustainability, visual arts, and more.
www.nshss.org

Peerlift: Information about scholarships, internships, summer programs, and more gathered by students.
www.peerlift.org

Scholar Snapp: Free data standard allowing students to reuse their application information for multiple scholarship applications.
www.scholarsnapp.org

Scholarships.com: Free website to search for college scholarship and financial aid information.

/www.scholarships.com

Scholarship America: Research and apply for scholarships from this website.

https://scholarshipamerica.org

Scholly: Mobile app to find scholarships for college.

https://myscholly.com

Thurgood Marshall College Fund: Provides scholarships for students at any of the forty-seven public historically black colleges and universities (HBCUs), as well as support for the institutions. Occasionally offers scholarships to students at other schools.

www.tmcf.org

UNCF: Awards scholarships and internships to students from low- and moderate-income families for college tuition, books, and room and board. Their website also has great tips on applying for other scholarships.

https://uncf.org

Apprenticeships

Apprenticeship.gov is the U.S. Department of Labor's website covering all things apprenticeship! Check out the whole site, but don't miss these important pages:

- **Jump Start Your Career through Apprenticeship**
  www.apprenticeship.gov/become-apprentice
  Everything you need to know to get started on an apprenticeship
- **Industry-Recognized Apprenticeship Program (IRAP)**
  www.apprenticeship.gov/employers/industry-recognized-apprenticeship-program
  Explains the criteria for apprenticeship programs to meet the U.S. Department of Labor's standards, such as including a paid-work component and an educational component. IRAPs are developed/delivered by trade and industry groups, corporations, nonprofit organizations, educational institutions, unions, and/or joint labor-management organizations.

Pre-Apprenticeship and Other Gateway Programs

IBEW (International Brotherhood of Electrical Workers) Pre-Apprenticeship Program

www.ibew.org/Civic-and-Community-Engagement/Pre-Apprenticeships

Local unions and IBEW/NECA training centers in the United States and Canada offer pre-apprenticeship programs to expand access to IBEW and extend opportunity beyond traditional demographic and regional borders. Introductory courses are designed to help those interested in a full apprenticeship develop skills and knowledge needed to enter the trades. Many programs offer direct entry into an apprenticeship upon successful completion.

Licensing and Other Regulations

NCCER (National Center for Construction Education and Research)

www.nccer.org

"A leader in workforce development for the construction industry, NCCER sets and maintains the global standard in construction training and certification. NCCER qualifications have been developed by CEOs and academic leaders to help learners gain credentials that are recognized by the industry around the world."

NCCER Craft Licensing Map provides information about licensing and reciprocity for the states that license electricians.

www.nccer.org/workforce-development-programs/reciprocity-map

Safety

OSHA (Occupational Safety and Health Administration) has put out a series of worker safety publications that are available online.

Construction: OSHA 3252-05N 2005 has some great information about the hazards that can be found on construction sites, how to protect yourself, and how to help keep accidents from happening. You can find it online at www.osha.gov/Publications/OSHA3252/3252.html.

State Licensing Boards

Alabama Electrical Contractors Board, www.aecb.state.al.us
Alaska: Professional Licensing, www.commerce.alaska.gov/web/cbpl
Arizona Registrar of Contractors, https://roc.az.gov
Arkansas: State of Arkansas Contractor's Licensing Board, www.aclb.arkansas.gov
California Contractors License Board, www.cslb.ca.gov
Colorado State Electrical Board, https://dpo.colorado.gov/Electrical
Connecticut: Department of Consumer Protection, https://portal.ct.gov/dcp
Delaware: Board of Electrical Examiners, https://dpr.delaware.gov/boards/electrician
District of Columbia: Department of Consumer and Regulatory Affairs, https://dcra.dc.gov
Florida: Electrical Contractors Licensing Board, www.myfloridalicense.com/DBPR/electrical-contractors
Georgia Board of Electrical Contractors, https://sos.ga.gov/index.php/licensing/plb/21
Hawaii: Board of Electricians and Plumbers, http://cca.hawaii.gov/pvl/boards/electrician
Idaho Division of Building Safety—Electrical Board, https://dbs.idaho.gov/boards/EBboard/members.html
Illinois Department of Financial and Professional Regulation, www.idfpr.com
Indiana Professional Licensing Agency, www.in.gov/pla
Iowa: Electrical Licensing and Inspection Program, https://dps.iowa.gov/divisions/state-fire-marshal/electrical-examining-board
Kansas Board of Technical Professions, www.ksbtp.ks.gov
Kentucky: OHB&C Electrical Division, http://dhbc.ky.gov
Louisiana State Licensing Board for Contractors, www.lslbc.louisiana.gov
Maine: Electrician's Examining Board, www.maine.gov/pfr/professionallicensing/professions/electricians/index.html

Maryland: State Board of Master Electricians, www.dllr.state.md.us/license/elec
Massachusetts: Board of State Examiners of Electricians, www.mass.gov/orgs/board-of-state-examiners-of-electricians
Michigan: Licensing and Regulatory Affairs, Electrical Division, www.michigan.gov/lara/0,4601,7-154-89334_10575_17394_77372-42954—,00.html
Minnesota: Electrical Licensing and Inspection, www.dli.mn.gov/workers/electricians-and-electrical-installers
Mississippi State Board of Contractors, www.msboc.us
Missouri Division of Professional Registration, https://pr.mo.gov/electricalcontractors-FAQ-Contractors.asp
Montana: State Electrical Board, http://boards.bsd.dli.mt.gov/ele
Nebraska State Electrical Board, https://electrical.nebraska.gov
Nevada State Contractors Board, www.nvcontractorsboard.com
New Hampshire: OPLC Electricians Board, www.oplc.nh.gov/electricians/index.htm
New Jersey: Board of Examiners of Electrical Contractors, www.njconsumer-affairs.gov/elec
New Mexico Regulation and Licensing Department, Construction Industries Division: Electrical Bureau, www.rld.state.nm.us/construction/electrical.aspx
New York: *New York doesn't license electricians at the state level.*
North Carolina State Board of Examiners of Electrical Contractors, www.ncbeec.org
North Dakota State Electrical Board, www.ndseb.com
Ohio Construction Industry Licensing Board, www.com.ohio.gov/dico/OCILB
Oklahoma State Construction Industries Board (Electrical), https://cib.ok.gov/electrical
Oregon: Electrical and Elevator Board, www.oregon.gov/bcd/boards/Pages/elec-elev.aspx
Pennsylvania Department of Labor and Industry, www.dli.pa.gov/Pages/default.aspx
Rhode Island Department of Labor and Training, Electricians, https://dlt.ri.gov/wrs/professionalregulation/electricians.php
South Carolina Labor Licensing Regulation, https://llr.sc.gov
South Dakota Electrical Commission, https://dlr.sd.gov/electrical/default.aspx

Tennessee Department of Commerce and Insurance, Limited Licensed Electricians, www.tn.gov/commerce/regboards/lle.html

Texas Department of Licensing and Regulation, www.tdlr.texas.gov

Utah Division of Occupational and Professional Licensing, Electrical, https://dopl.utah.gov/el/index.html

Vermont Electrical Licensing Board, https://firesafety.vermont.gov/licensing/electrical/board

Virginia DPOR Board for Contractors, www.dpor.virginia.gov/Boards/Contractors

Washington State Department of Labor and Industries, Electrical Program, https://lni.wa.gov/licensing-permits/electrical/electrical-licensing-exams-education

West Virginia: Office of the State Fire Marshal, Electrical Licensing, https://firemarshal.wv.gov/Divisions/Fire%20Services/Pages/Electrical-Licensing.aspx

Wisconsin Dept of Safety and Professional Service, Electrical Apprentice, https://dsps.wi.gov/Pages/Professions/ElectricalApprentice/Default.aspx

Wyoming Department of Fire Prevention and Electrical Safety, http://wsfm.wyo.gov/electrical-safety

Trade Associations and Organizations

American Solar Energy Society (ASES)

www.ases.org

ASES is a solar power association established in 1954 to advocate for sustainable living and renewable energy. It's an American association with an international reach. It offers conferences, training and other resources, and publishes *SolarToday Magazine.*

American Subcontractors Association (ASA)

www.asaonline.com

ASA "promotes the rights and interests of subcontractors, specialty contractors and suppliers." It provides education, events, news, and advocacy as well as members-only resources. It has chapters in all fifty states and the District of Columbia.

American Wind Energy Association (AWEA)
www.awea.org

AWEA is an association for the U.S. wind industry. Members have access to market information, resources, education, advocacy, and industry news.

Associated Builders and Contractors (ABC)
www.abc.org

With sixty-five chapters throughout the country, ABC is the largest construction association in the United States. It provides advocacy, education and training, networking, safety information, various types of insurance, and a national student chapter network.

Federated Electrical Contractors (FEC)
www.fec.org

The FEC is an international association with offices in sixty cities around the world. It focuses on joint ventures that bring electrical contractors together with specialized resources.

Independent Electrical Contractors (IEC)
www.ieci.org

The IEC focuses on independent contractors. They focus on training, management education, and workforce development. Members also have access to national meetings and other networking opportunities, advocacy, codes and safety information and representation, and various tools, resources, and discounts.

International Brotherhood of Electrical Workers (IBEW)
www.ibew.org

IBEW is a trade union for electricians. With more than 775,000 active members in fields in which electricians work (utilities, construction, telecommunications, broadcasting, manufacturing, railroads, and government), IBEW is one of the largest unions in America. IBEW bargains collectively with employers regarding wages, benefits, and rights. It also maintains a local union director, construction jobs board, and important forms and services for members. It also offers a pre-apprenticeship program. From the IBEW website:

"Most of us have very limited bargaining power as one person, but as a group, we are strong. And, with a good negotiated contract, we have legal protections we would not have otherwise."

National Association of Home Builders (NAHB)
www.nahb.org

NAHB is for tradespeople who work in residential construction. It provides members with education and training, networking, business solutions expertise, advocacy, and discounts.

National Electrical Contractors Association (NECA)
www.necanet.org

One of the largest associations specifically dedicated to the electrical contracting industry. Member benefits include education and training, advocacy and representation, business and market development, networking and events, and various discounts, tools, resources, and services.

Smart Electric Power Alliance (SEPA)
https://sepapower.org

SEPA is focused on creating a clean and modern electrical grid. Members have access to networking, discounts, trade shows, education and training, business development support, and member-only content.

U.S. Green Building Council (USGBC)
www.usgbc.org

USGBC oversees LEED (Leadership in Energy and Environmental Design) certification. Members have access to LEED courses and credential maintenance webinars, a listing in their directory, discounts, and members-only information and publications.

Bibliography

Adkins, William. "How to Get Certified as a Residential Electrician." *Chron*. Updated February 12, 2019. https://work.chron.com/certified-residential-electrician-14017.html.

Bureau of Labor Statistics (BLS). "Occupational Employment Statistics. Occupational Employment and Wages, May 2019; 47-2111 Electricians." www.bls.gov/oes/current/oes472111.htm#st.

———. "Occupational Outlook Handbook—Electrical and Electronics Installers and Repairers." Last modified September 1, 2020. www.bls.gov/ooh/installation-maintenance-and-repair/electrical-and-electronics-installers-and-repairers.htm#tab-1.

———. "Occupational Outlook Handbook—Electricians." www.bls.gov/ooh/construction-and-extraction/electricians.htm#tab-1.

———. "Occupational Outlook Handbook—Line Installers and Repairers/Summary." Last modified September 1, 2020. www.bls.gov/ooh/installation-maintenance-and-repair/line-installers-and-repairers.htm#tab-3.

College Choice. "Best Electrician Schools." 2020. www.collegechoice.net/rankings/best-electrician-schools.

College Consensus. "Best Trades Scholarships." 2020. www.collegeconsensus.com/scholarships/trade-school-scholarships.

Colorado Electrical Board. "Electrical Board: Continuing Education." https://dpo.colorado.gov/Electrical/CE.

———. "Electrician Licensure by Examination or Endorsement." https://dpo.colorado.gov/Electrical/Applications.

Consador, Kat. "The Salary of Power Lineman Jobs." *Career Trend*. Updated September 26, 2017. https://careertrend.com/the-salary-of-power-lineman-jobs-13637491.html.

ElectricianSchoolEdu. "State-by-State Electrician License and Certification Requirements at a Glance." www.electricianschooledu.org/state-by-state-licensing-guide.

Electrician Training Hub. "Electrician Levels/Ranks." https://electriciantraininghub.com/how-to-become-an-electrician/electrician-ranks.

GateWay Community College. "Constructions Trades: Electricity." www.gatewaycc.edu/degrees-certificates/applied-technology/construction-trades-electricity-3428-aas.

GoCollege. "Your Guide to Free Money: College Scholarships." www.gocollege.com/financial-aid/scholarships.

Griffin, Jeff. "Tools Most Used by Electricians." *Electrical Contractor.* January 2005. www.ecmag.com/section/your-business/tools-most-used-electricians.

Home Stratosphere. "23 Types of Electricians (Based on Specialization and Certifications)." www.homestratosphere.com/types-of-electricians.

IATSE Local 4. *Theatrical Electrician Handbook*. Brooklyn, NY: Theatrical Stage Employees, Local No.4, IATSE, 2011. www.iatselocal4.org/Docs/Study_Guides/Theatrical_Electrician_Handbook_Rev2.pdf.

IBEW. "Leveling the Playing Field: Pre-Apprenticeships Open Doors to the Middle Class." February 12, 2019. www.ibew.org/media-center/Articles/20Daily/2002/200212_Leveling.

———. "Pre-Apprenticeship Programs." 2020. www.ibew.org/Civic-and-Community-Engagement/Pre-Apprenticeships.

Kelly, Kate. "Vocational Education in High School: What You Need to Know." *Understood* Accessed August 19, 2019. www.understood.org/en/school-learning/choosing-starting-school/finding-right-school/vocational-education-in-high-school.

Knox, Nora. "LEED: I've Got a Question! Taking a LEED Professional Exam." *U.S. Green Building Council.* May 29, 2014. www.usgbc.org/articles/ive-got-question-taking-leed-professional-exam.

Lee, Chris. "A Quick Rundown of Electrical Contracting Trade Associations." *Esticom*. February 17, 2017. www.esticom.com/quick-rundown-electrical-contracting-trade-associations.

Locsin, Aurelio. "What Is the Difference between an Electrician and Electrical Engineer?" *Career Trend.* Updated December 31, 2018. https://careertrend.com/difference-between-electrician-electrical-engineer-12215.html.

Ma, Jennifer, Sandy Baum, Matea Pender, and C. J. Libassi. *Trends in College Pricing 2019.* New York: College Board, 2019.

Manchester Community College. "Electrical Technology." www.mccnh.edu/academics/programs/electrical-technology.

Miller, Scott. "What Is a Low Voltage Electrician? (License and Training)." *Vocational Training HQ*. Last updated May 28, 2020. www.vocationaltraininghq.com/what-is-a-low-voltage-electrician.

Minnesota Board of Electricity. "Electrical Licensing Basics." www.dli.mn.gov/workers/electrician-or-electrical-installer/electrical-license-experience-and-education.

National Center for Construction Education and Research. "NCCER Craft Licensing Map." 2020. www.nccer.org/news-research/reciprocity-map.

National Fire Protection Association. *National Electrical Code, 2020*. Boston: Cengage, 2020.

Salt Lake Community College. "Electrician License Renewal." www.slcc.edu/continuinged/programs/electrician-license-renewal.aspx.

Samarasekera, Rukesh. "LEED Credits, Prerequisites, and Points: How Are They Different?" *U.S. Green Building Council*. March 6, 2017. www.usgbc.org/articles/whats-difference-between-leed-credit-leed-prerequisite-and-leed-point.

Schnute, Steve. "Electrician Tools: A Master List." *Ask the Electrical Guy*. https://asktheelectricalguy.com/electrician-tools-list.

———. "How to Become an Electrician: Complete 5-Step Guide." *Ask the Electrical Guy*. https://asktheelectricalguy.com/how-to-become-an-electrician.

South Dakota Electrical Commission. "Licensing." 2020. https://dlr.sd.gov/electrical/licensing.aspx.

Staci, Kristel. "Electrical Design Principles for LEED Building Design." *Blue and Green Tomorrow*. July 11, 2018. https://blueandgreentomorrow.com/environment/electrical-design-principles-leed-building-design.

StateCE Blog. "Types of Electricians." May 4, 2018. www.statece.com/blog/profession/types-of-electricians.

Stoval, Qyou. "High Voltage Electrician Job Description." *Career Trend*. Updated October 25, 2019. https://careertrend.com/about-6060410-high-voltage-electrician-job-description.html.

Tesla, Nikola. "The Transmission of Electrical Energy without Wires as a Means for Furthering Peace." *Electrical World and Engineer*. January 7, 1905. www.tfcbooks.com/tesla/1905-01-07.htm.

Texas Department of Licensing and Regulation. "Electrician Continuing Education." www.tdlr.texas.gov/electricians/elecce.htm.

U.S. Department of Labor. "Industry-Recognized Apprenticeship Program." www.apprenticeship.gov/employers/industry-recognized-apprenticeship-program.

———. "Jump Start Your Career through Apprenticeship." www.apprenticeship.gov/become-apprentice.

U.S. Department of Labor Employment and Training Administration. "U.S. Department of Labor Issues Industry-Recognized Apprenticeship Program Final Rule." March 10, 2020. Press release # 20-386-NAT. www.dol.gov/newsroom/releases/eta/eta20200310.

U.S. Small Business Administration. "Review Common Business Structures." www.sba.gov/business-guide/launch-your-business/choose-business-structure#section-header-1.

Vermont Department of Public Safety, Division of Fire Safety. "Frequently Asked Questions." https://firesafety.vermont.gov/fire-building-safety/boards/electrical/faq.

Vermont General Assembly. "The Vermont Statutes Online: 26 V.S.A. § 905. Application; Examinations and Fees." https://legislature.vermont.gov/statutes/section/26/015/00905.

Wikiquote. "Thomas Edison." https://en.wikiquote.org/wiki/Thomas_Edison.

Wyoming Department of Fire Prevention and Electrical Safety. "Master Electrician Exam." https://drive.google.com/file/d/1l_LnqZWlyKjNSxGAcA42gyezSZzNmXRN/view.

Yochim, Dayana, and Andrea Coombes. "Best Retirement Plans: Choose the Right Account for You." *Nerdwallet*. September 4, 2020. www.nerdwallet.com/blog/investing/best-retirement-plans-for-you.

About the Author

Marcia Santore is an author and artist from New England. She enjoys writing about interesting people and the fascinating things they do. She's written on many topics, including profiles of artists, scholars, scientists, and businesspeople. She has also illustrated and published several children's books. See her writing website at www.amalgamatedstory.com and her artwork at www.marciasantore.com.

EDITORIAL BOARD

Eric Evitts has been working with teens in the high school setting for twenty-three years. Most of his career has dealt with getting teens, especially at-risk students, to find and follow a career path of interest. He has developed curriculum for Frederick County Public Schools focusing on anti-bullying and career development. He is currently a counselor at South Hagerstown High School.

Danielle Irving-Johnson, MA, EdS, is currently the career services specialist at the American Counseling Association. She exercises her specialty in career counseling by providing career guidance, services, and resources designed to encourage and assist students and professionals in obtaining their educational, employment, and career goals while also promoting the importance of self-care, wellness, work-life balance, and burnout prevention. Danielle has also previously served as a mental health counselor and clinical intake assessor in community agency settings assisting diverse populations with various diagnoses.

Joyce Rhine Shull, BS, MS, is an active member of the Maryland Association of Community College's Career Affinity Group and the Maryland Career Development Association. She presently serves as an academic advisor in higher education and teaches professionalism in the workplace as an adjunct professor. Her experience also includes two decades of management and career education of vocational courses and seminars for high school students.

Lisa Adams Somerlot is the president of the American College Counseling Association and also serves as director of counseling at the University of West Georgia. She has a PhD in counselor education from Auburn University and is a licensed professional counselor in Georgia and a nationally approved clinical supervisor. She is certified in Myers Briggs Type Indicator Strong Interest Inventory and in Strengths Quest administration.